Fabio's
AMERICAN
HOME KITCHEN

ALSO BY FABIO VIVIANI

Fabio's Italian Kitchen

hachette BOOKS

New York   Boston

FABIO VIVIANI

PHOTOGRAPHS BY MATT ARMENDARIZ

Fabio's AMERICAN HOME KITCHEN

More Than 125 RECIPES
With an Italian Accent

Hachette Books
Hachette Book Group
1290 Avenue of the Americas
New York, NY 10104

www.HachetteBookGroup.com

Printed in the United States of America

Q-MA

First Edition: October 2014
10 9 8 7 6 5 4 3 2 1

Hachette Books is a division of Hachette Book
Group, Inc.
The Hachette Books name and logo are trademarks
of Hachette Book Group, Inc.

The Hachette Speakers Bureau provides a wide
range of authors for speaking events. To find out
more, go to www.hachettespeakersbureau.com or
call (866) 376-6591.

The publisher is not responsible for websites (or their
content) that are not owned by the publisher.

Library of Congress Cataloging-in-Publication Data
Viviani, Fabio.
   Fabio's American home kitchen : more than 125
recipes with an Italian accent /
Fabio Viviani ; photographs by Matt Armendariz.—
First edition.
      pages   cm
   Includes bibliographical references and index.
   ISBN 978-1-4013-1284-8 (hardcover)—ISBN
978-1-4013-3083-5 (ebook) 1. Cooking, Italian.
2. Cooking, American. I. Title. II. Title: American
home kitchen.
TX723.V5788 2014
641.5945—dc23   2014011059

To the love of my life, Ashley, and to the best bed hog I could ever ask for, my dog Neiman. I live, breathe, and cook for you guys. This book is dedicated to you.

CONTENTS

INTRODUCTION

AMERICA! YOU GUYS HAVE so many different types of food! So I decided to write a book exploring the country and spend some time highlighting different cultures and the food that fuels them. In case you didn't know, I'm Italian to the core. My blood bleeds red, white, and green and I'm pretty sure my bones are fortified with al dente pasta. But that doesn't mean that I write off other cultures and their food. From flavor-forward Mexican cuisine to corner store southern Italian *bottega*, I want to dive into it all and immerse myself.

From Chicago and New York to Los Angeles and San Francisco, America lets everyone live out their culture through food. That's why I can walk down a street and see Thai food on my left, and a hamburger shop on my right. And only in America will these two maybe get together to form Thai burgers! The possibilities are endless and I draw inspiration from them. Don't get me wrong—I love my grandma's and mother's Italian cooking. But when I can start with an idea from them, and integrate something I might've seen while traveling, it takes it to another level. It's never about re-inventing the wheel—just making it spin faster and more deliciously than it did before.

American seafood alone is enough to knock me out: California has its local varieties of sea bass, South Carolina its juicy shrimp, then travel north and find Maine serving its prize catch of lobster. This stuff is good, guys. Trust me!

Head to southern Louisiana for a taste of something spicy in New Orleans, then hop over to Texas for arguably the best handmade tortilla in the country. It's crazy to think that each state has anywhere from ten to fifteen different cultures occupying it and bringing their food along for the ride.

Gone are the days of "this place has the best (insert food here)." Yes, some places are more well-known than others for their cuisine, but it comes down to the people that make it. If you have a Memphis native living in North Dakota, he takes his knowledge of making ribs with him and, all of a sudden, North Dakota has unreal Memphis-style ribs! Never underestimate this country and the people in it. I'm not the first one to say that America is a melting pot. All you have to do is make sure to keep the flame low, stir it every now and then, and season to taste. You will get a new and exciting flavor every time you dip your spoon in.

1

FABIO'S KITCHEN NOTES

Assumptions and Some Common Sense

FIRST OF ALL, I am assuming that everyone has a small kitchen scale, and if you don't have a scale, buy one! I will leave items that you buy at the store in ounces and pounds as is. Don't worry—I will not send you to the store asking for 3 cups of cream cheese, just like I won't ask you to use 3 cups of canned crushed tomatoes when you buy those in ounces.

Now, here are some basic guidelines for using the recipes in this book.

All flour is all-purpose unless otherwise specified.

All eggs are large unless otherwise specified.

All sugar is regular white granulated unless otherwise specified.

All salt is kosher or coarse unless otherwise specified.

Pepper is always freshly ground black pepper unless otherwise specified.

All red wine should be dry and something that you'd be happy drinking, not bad wine, or anything labeled "cooking wine."

Chicken stock is always preferably homemade, but if you use store-bought it should be organic and low-sodium.

Mayonnaise is also always preferably homemade, though nothing will happen to you if you use store-bought.

All dairy products are full fat unless otherwise specified.

Cooking heat on the stove is always medium unless otherwise specified.

Olive oil is always extra-virgin unless otherwise specified.

Butter is always unsalted unless otherwise specified.

Pasta is dried unless otherwise specified.

Common Sense

Common sense always applies in the kitchen and will help you a lot more than just following recipes precisely, so try to train your powers of observation and use your common sense as you cook. Here are a few basic tips on that front:

When chefs—including me!—say to cook something "until caramelized, about 15 minutes," they're thinking about *their* stove, *their* fire, *their* pots and pans. At *your* house, you need to cook it until it *looks* caramelized. That's why you're much better off understanding what "caramelized" means rather than walking away for fifteen minutes and coming back to a disaster. What do I mean when I say caramelized? Vegetables release water, and you'll see that, too, in the form of a very light steam. Caramelized is the next step after that. All the moisture has disappeared, the vegetables will start to brown lightly on the edges, and the bottom of the pan has little brown bits here and there. In order to caramelize, vegetables have to touch the bottom of the pan and the oil or butter if you're us-

ing any. *Heat* has to be there, and because anything you cook has to have contact with the bottom of your cooking vessel, when you use a wider sauté pan, caramelizing takes less time than when you use a taller pot with a smaller diameter bottom. I don't know how long it's going to take in *your* pan because I don't know what pan you have!

Seasoning is not a science with rules set in stone. If you like food not too salty then use less. If, like me, you like food really well seasoned then add about 25 percent more salt than these recipes call for. Do you like a lot of pepper? Great! Add more. Do you hate paprika? Take it away. It's that simple.

I often say pasta should be cooked in salted boiling water. What I mean by that is about a gallon of water and a handful of salt. If you have a hand that is big like a sumo wrestler's head, then maybe you only need half a handful of salt. But if you have the hand of a three-year-old, then you probably need two handfuls of salt. See what I mean? (And for the record, a handful of salt is usually 2 to 3 tablespoons).

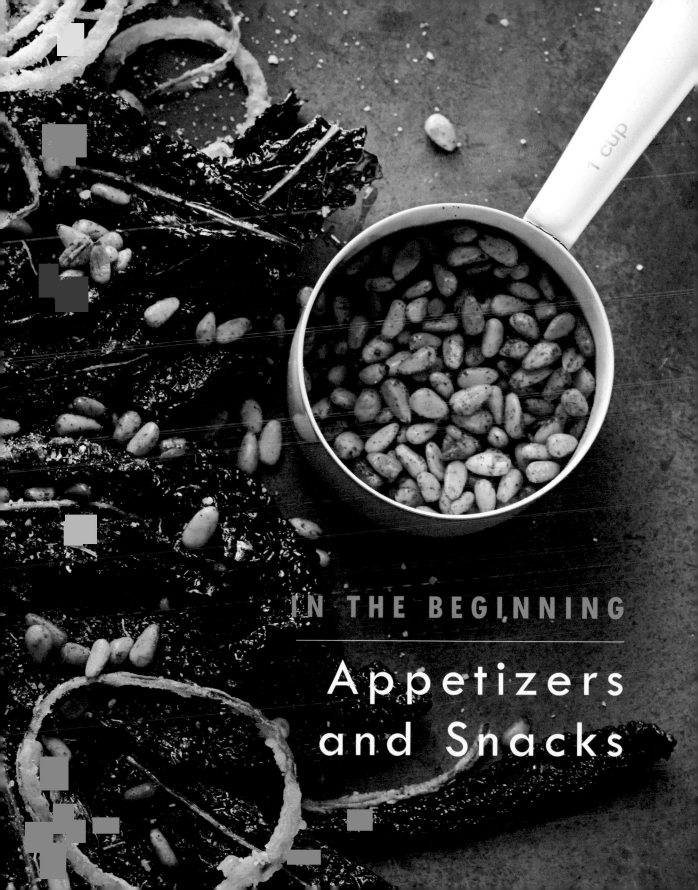

IN THE BEGINNING

Appetizers
and Snacks

WHAT BETTER WAY TO START YOUR EVENING OF DINING THAN with a little taste of something wonderful? Appetizers are the "first kiss" of your meal and should set the tempo for the rest of the night and spark interest, conversation, smiles, and laughs. Pair them with a cocktail and let the games begin.

As for size, remember these recipes are just a small dish or couple of bites to stimulate your appetite. Anything more than that and you'll be too full to enjoy the rest of the meal. The kind of meal you're serving should determine what kind of "apps" are going to be served. If it's for a big game or other event, focus on dips and things that can sit out on platters on the table at room temperature like chips, savory biscuiti, crackers, and bruschette. If it's something a little fancier, like a pre-wedding lunch, think sandwiches, small pastries, and spreads with light flavors and textures. A bigger bash calls for things like chilled and smoked seafood or canapés, and since I'm not French, cold cuts and larger pieces of toasted bread with a variety of ingredients as topping will do the work. Or, if you're welcoming people to your home for the first time, try baked things that will make the place smell fantastic.

Of course the best reason to make appetizers is for a family dinner. Nobody is judging you here so go for comfort food like stuffed vegetables and breads and lots of it. Put it on platters and let everyone go at it with their knives and forks.

Spicy Zucchini, Squash, Ricotta, and Mint Salad

This salad is super refreshing and perfect for a cool summer night. Because the zucchini squash are cooked, they keep the temperature of the dish a little warm.

Wash and cut each zucchini lengthwise in half, remove the seeds with a spoon, cut the halves into quarters, then cut each quarter into strips about ⅛ inch wide. Coarsely chop the endives.

In a large pan, heat the olive oil. Add the garlic and sauté until golden brown, about 1 minute.

Add the zucchini and the endive and stir quickly. Season with salt and pepper. When the zucchini are cooked but still firm, 3 to 4 minutes, transfer the mixture to a large plate to cool.

Roughly chop the mint and basil, place in a large bowl, and add the zucchini, arugula, and jalapeño. Toss well and season with lemon juice and olive oil. Dollop the ricotta over the top of the salad and serve.

4 medium yellow zucchini squash

4 medium green zucchini

3 Belgian endives

2 tablespoons extra-virgin olive oil plus more for dressing the salad

2 garlic cloves, crushed

Kosher salt and freshly ground black pepper

1 bunch fresh mint, washed, dried, stems removed

1 bunch fresh basil, washed, dried, stems removed

1 pound arugula, well washed and dried

1 jalapeño pepper, seeds and ribs removed, thinly sliced

Juice of ½ lemon

1½ cups ricotta cheese

Kale Salad with Mushrooms, Mozzarella, and Orange Segments

This salad has great versatility. Feel free to swap out any citrus fruit in season—grapefruit, blood oranges, tangerines, mandarin oranges, and even limes can be used. Let your palate go wild!

Heat the oil in a sauté pan over medium heat, add the mushrooms, and cook until they are crisp, 8 to10 minutes. Season with salt and pepper to taste, remove from heat, and set aside.

In a small bowl, combine the Parmesan, vinegar, and garlic and whisk together until thoroughly mixed.

Put the kale, sun-dried tomatoes, oranges, and mozzarella in a large bowl and toss to combine. Add the cooked mushrooms to the top, then drizzle with the dressing and serve immediately.

3 tablespoons olive oil

1 pound oyster mushrooms, cleaned and roughly chopped

Kosher salt and freshly ground black pepper

½ cup grated Parmesan cheese

2 tablespoons balsamic vinegar

1 garlic clove, finely chopped

1½ pounds kale, tough ribs removed, leaves roughly chopped

6 ounces sun-dried tomatoes, preferably Fabio's recipe (page 13), roughly chopped (if you use store-bought sun-dried tomatoes packed in oil, squeeze out as much oil as you can)

6 ounces orange segments (the canned ones from the store are fine, or you can prepare your own)

6 ounces shredded fresh mozzarella cheese

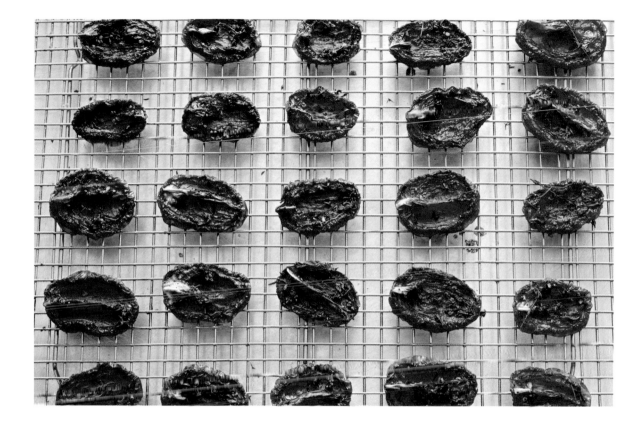

MAKES ABOUT 1½ POUNDS

Fabio's Sun-dried Tomatoes

3 pounds plum tomatoes, halved and seeds squeezed out

2 tablespoons extra-virgin olive oil

½ cup chopped fresh thyme

1 tablespoon kosher salt

1 tablespoon freshly ground black pepper

Put all the ingredients into a metal bowl, mix well, and let rest for about 1 hour. The tomatoes will release water.

Preheat the oven to 225°F.

Place a wire rack on a sheet pan, then place the tomato halves on the rack, cut side up. Roast for about 7 hours.

Use immediately or store, covered in olive oil, in a mason jar in your fridge.

Crostini and Bruschette

Pick and choose between these different toppings according to what you prefer, but a crusty piece of sliced bread is always the best pick for an appetizer! No canapés here—Italians need bread (even if we have to settle for a baguette). You can make the slices smaller or bigger, thinner or thicker, depending on your topping, and you can use these recipes to make 10 or 100, depending on how many people you want to feed.

Crostini and bruschette are very similar, but crostini are normally smaller and not necessarily grilled or toasted, while bruschette are wider, more rustic, and usually grilled and served with a drizzle of olive oil. Anything that you would eat in a sandwich can be part of the topping for either one—these are just a few examples of what can be done.

Basic Crostini

Sliced baguette or other crusty
    bread
Extra-virgin olive oil
Sea salt
White pepper ground from a
    peppermill

Preheat the oven to 425°F.

    Arrange the sliced bread on a baking sheet and season each piece with a good drizzle of olive oil, some sea salt, and a good grind of white pepper.

    Bake for 4 to 5 minutes until the edges of the bread start to turn dark brown (a little bit of black is OK).

Garlic cloves (depending on
    how many you're making),
    peeled and whole.

Garlic Variation:
Follow the basic instructions, rubbing each slice of bread with garlic before adding the salt and pepper.

---

1 (or more, depending on how
    many you're making) whole
    ripe tomato, cut in half

Tomato Variation:
Follow the basic instructions. Once the crostini are out of the oven, squeeze the tomato halves, open side down, over the slices. Really good, really fresh tomato purée!

Grated Parmesan cheese
    (amount depends on how
    many you make)

Parmesan Variation:
Follow the garlic crostini instructions. Once the crostini are out of the oven, dust the surface of each slice with some of the Parmesan.

Pesto (store-bought or see
    recipe, page 40)
Extra-virgin olive oil

Pesto Variation:
Follow the basic instructions. Once the crostini are out of the oven, add 1 to 2 tablespoons of pesto to each slice according to taste, then drizzle with olive oil.

Grilled Asparagus with Burrata and Almond Salsa

1 pound blanched asparagus (bottom 1 inch peeled if using large spears)

16 ounces burrata cheese, cut into eighths

Kosher salt and freshly ground black pepper

¼ cup extra-virgin olive oil

1 teaspoon finely grated lemon zest

1 tablespoon fresh lemon juice

1 tablespoon fresh lime juice

1 tablespoon honey

1 tablespoon balsamic vinegar

½ cup coarsely chopped almonds

10 to 15 whole basil leaves

If you're using larger asparagus for this, be sure to peel the bottom inch (but no need to cut it off). To blanch the asparagus, bring a big pot of salted water to a boil, then drop in the spears. One minute of blanching is enough for the thinner ones, about 5 minutes for the larger ones.

Set up a bowl of cold water and ice cubes. Once the asparagus are done, transfer them immediately to the ice bath and let them cool completely before you grill them, or they will turn to mush (don't worry about drying them—this will happen instantly on the grill).

Burrata is a fresh Italian cheese, a shell of mozzarella enclosing a filling of cream and bits of soft curds. It's like the love child of mozzarella and mascarpone.

Heat a grill to high and place the asparagus on it. Grill, turning the spears, until the asparagus is charred on all sides, about 10 minutes.

Transfer the asparagus to a serving platter and immediately top with the burrata, so it begins to melt.

Combine the salt, pepper, olive oil, lemon zest, lemon juice, lime juice, honey, balsamic vinegar, and almonds in a bowl and mix together. Drizzle the mixture over the burrata with a spoon, and season with additional salt and pepper to taste.

Garnish with basil leaves and serve.

Roasted Apricot Tapenade

SERVES 6 TO 8

This makes a perfect topping for bruschetta and also works well as a sauce or side for any roasted meat.

Preheat the oven to 425°F.

Place the apricot halves in a baking dish, cut side up, and drizzle them with 3 tablespoons of olive oil. Roast them in the oven for 10 minutes, then set aside to cool.

Place the rosemary, lemon juice, garlic, salt, pepper, pine nuts, and basil leaves in a food processor fitted with the blade and process until they become a paste. If the mixture becomes too dry, add the remaining olive oil, one tablespoon at a time, until it reaches the desired consistency. Transfer the mixture to a bowl, roughly chop the cooled apricots, and fold them into the tapenade.

To store, keep the tapenade refrigerated, covered with a thin layer of olive oil. It will keep for about a week.

10 hard apricots, halved and pitted
½ cup plus 3 tablespoons extra-virgin olive oil
2 rosemary sprigs, needles removed, stems discarded
Juice of ½ lemon
1 garlic clove
Kosher salt and freshly ground black pepper
1 cup pine nuts
20 fresh basil leaves

Spinach and Goat Cheese Butter Buns with Nuts

1 whole egg plus 1 egg yolk

⅔ cup milk

2⅓ cups flour

1 package active dry yeast (2¼ teaspoons)

Pinch of kosher salt

1 teaspoon freshly ground black pepper

½ pound (2 sticks) cold butter, cut into cubes

1 cup pine nuts

8 ounces spinach; if fresh, large stems removed and roughly chopped; if frozen, thawed and squeezed dry

⅓ cup chopped walnuts

6 ounces goat cheese, crumbled

S oft, just-baked bread out of the oven is a thing of beauty, and the cheese flavor and the crunch of the nuts really set this one apart.

In a small bowl, whisk together the egg, egg yolk, and milk.

In a food processor, combine the flour, yeast, salt, pepper, and butter and pulse until the mixture comes together into small pieces. Add the milk and egg mixture and ½ cup of the pine nuts, and pulse for another minute.

Cover the processor bowl with plastic wrap and place it in the refrigerator for at least 4 hours, and preferably overnight. Remove the dough from the refrigerator; it should have risen by about half. Punch down the dough to flatten it and divide it into 6 equal balls.

Preheat the oven to 350°F and oil a 6-cup muffin pan.

Sauté the spinach in a dry pan over medium heat until its liquid has released and evaporated. Add the walnuts and the remaining ½ cup pine nuts, and stir to combine.

Place the dough balls in the prepared muffin pan and distribute the mixture evenly over the buns. Crumble the goat cheese over the top, and set aside to rise again in a warm, draft-free place for 1 hour and 15 minutes.

Bake the buns until golden brown, about 30 minutes. Remove from the muffin pans and serve warm.

Fava Bean–Mint Hummus

MAKES 2 TO 3 CUPS;
ENOUGH FOR
4 TO 6 PEOPLE

It's time to step away from the plain garbanzos! Here's a different spin on hummus, packed with untraditional flavors and nutrients.

Add the baking soda to a medium pot of salted water and bring to a boil. Add the fava beans and cook for 5 minutes. Drain the beans.

Put the fava beans, chickpeas, Parmesan, garlic, olive oil, mint, and sour cream into the bowl of a food processor fitted with the blade and pulse until you have a coarse paste. Store the hummus in the refrigerator, covered, for up to 1 week. Serve with a good drizzle of extra-virgin olive oil on top.

1 teaspoon baking soda

2½ cups frozen shelled fava beans, or fresh if in season

1 cup canned garbanzo beans (chickpeas), rinsed and drained

½ cup grated Parmesan cheese

2 garlic cloves

½ cup extra-virgin olive oil

3 tablespoons fresh mint leaves, chopped

1 cup sour cream

Hazelnut, Lemon, and Parmesan Biscotti

If you like biscotti, you'll enjoy this savory version. Try serving them as a side dish, instead of bread, for appetizers, or with an herbal tea for an afternoon snack.

Preheat the oven to 340°F. Line a half sheet pan (13 × 18 inches) with parchment paper.

In a large bowl, combine the salt, baking soda, and flour. In a separate bowl, beat the whole eggs with a fork. Continue beating and add the sugar, vanilla, lemon zest, and olive oil.

Add 1 tablespoon of milk to the bowl with the dry ingredients and mix, then add additional milk, one tablespoon at a time, if the dough is too dry. Mix in the grated cheese and the chopped nuts. Cut the dough in half, and shape each piece into a rectangle with smooth edges. Place the pieces, slightly separated, onto the lined sheet pan. Beat the egg yolks and brush them over the dough so it is completely coated.

Bake for 25 to 30 minutes, or until golden brown.

Remove the dough from the pan and, using a serrated knife, cut each piece into 10 equal slices. Return the slices to the baking pan and bake for another 5 to 6 minutes on each side until the biscotti are golden brown. Turn the oven off, and leave the pan with the cookies in the oven until they are completely cool.

The biscotti can be stored in an airtight container for 1 week.

½ teaspoon kosher salt

½ teaspoon baking soda

1⅔ cups bread flour

2 whole eggs plus 2 egg yolks

½ cup sugar

2 teaspoons pure vanilla extract

Finely grated zest of 3 lemons

¼ cup extra-light olive oil

¼ cup milk

½ cup grated Parmesan cheese

1 cup hazelnuts, coarsely chopped

Rosemary and Pecorino Shortbread

10 tablespoons (1¼ sticks) butter plus more for the pan

¼ cup sugar

1 tablespoon honey

1⅔ cups flour plus additional for dusting

2 teaspoons baking powder

¼ cup finely chopped fresh rosemary leaves

Pinch of kosher salt

2 tablespoons grated pecorino Romano cheese

10 sun-dried tomatoes (page 13), cut into small pieces (if you use store-bought sun-dried tomatoes packed in oil, squeeze out as much oil as you can)

Extra-virgin olive oil, for drizzling (optional)

For a more intense herb aroma, sprinkle the tops of the shortbread with some chopped thyme and rosemary as soon as they come out of the oven.

Preheat the oven to 340°F. Grease a 9-inch round cake pan.

In a large bowl, beat the butter, sugar, and honey to a creamy consistency.

Stir in the flour, baking powder, rosemary, and salt. Dust the countertop generously with flour. Transfer the dough from the bowl to the countertop and knead it a few times until you have a smooth dough ball.

Press the dough evenly into the pan and divide it into 8 wedges with the dull edge of a knife. Prick holes in the dough with the tines of a fork and garnish each wedge with some grated cheese and a piece of sun-dried tomato.

Bake the shortbread for 15 to 20 minutes until light brown. Let cool in the pan for 10 minutes, then carefully remove it. If you'd like, drizzle the shortbread with olive oil just before serving.

Italian Fried Missouri-Style Ravioli

As if pasta could've gotten any better? This is the Holy Grail of comfort food.

Put the onion, garlic, and olive oil in a saucepan over medium heat and cook until the onion is nicely caramelized, 5 to 7 minutes. Stir in the tomatoes, crushing them with a wooden spoon as you add them. Add the basil and season with salt and pepper. Cook for another 10 minutes or so, until the tomatoes are soft, stirring just enough to keep them from burning on the bottom of the pan.

Stir in the tomato paste and bring the sauce to a boil. Reduce the heat to low and simmer until the tomatoes have completely broken down, 20 to 25 minutes.

In a small bowl, combine the eggs and milk. In a shallow bowl, mix together the bread crumbs and ½ cup of the grated cheese. Dip each ravioli into the egg mixture, then into the Parmesan bread crumbs to coat.

Heat the oil in an 8- to 9-inch deep sauté pan to 350°F. Add the ravioli, a few at a time, and fry for about 2 minutes, or until golden brown, turning them once. Using a slotted spoon, remove the ravioli from the hot oil and transfer to paper towels to drain. Sprinkle with the remaining Parmesan and serve hot with the dipping sauce on the side.

½ cup finely chopped onion

2 garlic cloves, minced

2 tablespoons olive oil

32 ounces canned plum tomatoes

2 tablespoons chopped fresh basil

Kosher salt and freshly ground black pepper

2 tablespoons tomato paste

2 eggs

½ cup milk

1½ cups panko bread crumbs

1 cup grated Parmesan cheese

1 pound small frozen cheese ravioli OR ½ recipe Fabio's Ricotta Ravioli (page 26)

4 to 5 cups light olive oil, for frying

— {Continued} —

Fabio's Ricotta Ravioli

MAKE THE FILLING: In a mixing bowl, thoroughly combine the ricotta, Parmesan, mozzarella, eggs, and salt and pepper. Chill in the refrigerator for at least a few minutes to firm up (it's fine to leave it in the fridge while you make the dough, too).

MAKE THE DOUGH: Place the eggs and egg yolks in a food processor fitted with the blade attachment, add the salt, pepper, and olive oil, and pulse a few times.

Add half of the flour and pulse until the eggs absorb it and you have a semi-thick paste. Add the rest of the flour and allow the blade to rotate continuously. When you see a ball-shaped mass of flour and eggs bouncing around the canister, the dough is ready. If the dough is still too wet to the touch, add an extra tablespoon of flour. If it is a bit dry, add a little water as needed, tablespoon by tablespoon.

Roll the dough out into two thin, 4 × 8-inch sheets. Place about 2 teaspoons of the filling every inch or so along the top half of each sheet. Then fold the bottom half of each sheet over the top half and press down gently around the edges of each blob of filling to seal it in and remove any air bubbles. Using a zigzag cutter, a knife, or cookie cutters in the shape of your choice, cut out the individual ravioli.

Gather up any dough scraps and roll them out again, and continue to make ravioli until you run out of filling.

Filling

1½ cups ricotta cheese, well drained
¼ cup grated Parmesan cheese
¼ cup shredded mozzarella cheese
2 eggs
Kosher salt and freshly ground black pepper

Dough

6 whole eggs plus 4 egg yolks
Pinch of kosher salt
½ teaspoon freshly ground black pepper
2 teaspoons olive oil
2 cups flour

The Best Salmon Candy from Alaska

2 cups granulated sugar

½ cup kosher salt

1 pound skinless Alaskan King salmon fillet, cut into ½-inch strips

⅓ cup pure maple syrup

2 tablespoons dark brown sugar

4 teaspoons soy sauce

1 teaspoon coarsely ground black pepper

In Alaska this is traditionally made with salmon, usually Chinook. I personally also use river trout, which is equally delicious.

Whisk the sugar and salt in a bowl. Spread out one-third of the mixture in a flat dish large enough to hold the salmon.

Place the salmon strips on top of the seasonings in one layer. Completely cover the strips with the remaining sugar-salt mixture. Cover the dish with plastic wrap and refrigerate for at least 12 hours, preferably longer.

Preheat the oven to 175°F. Remove the salmon strips from the curing salt and carefully scrape off as much as possible. Blot the salmon dry all over with paper towels. Arrange the salmon strips, spaced ½ inch apart, on a rack set on a parchment paper–lined baking sheet. Let the salmon air-dry at room temperature for 45 minutes.

Whisk together the maple syrup, brown sugar, and soy sauce in a bowl.

Put the salmon in the oven and brush every 30 minutes with the glaze. Keep doing this for about 5 hours. It's a little time-consuming, but totally worth it.

Sprinkle with the coarsely ground pepper 15 minutes after you remove it from the oven. It's ready for eating!

Kale Chips with Pecorino and Pine Nuts

A tasty spin on the kale-fever that is going around America and fun to eat, this is a showstopper at any party. You can also mix these with other leafy greens after the kale is fried for a more classic salad with a crunch.

Heat a tablespoon of oil in a large frying pan over medium-low heat. Add the pine nuts and sauté, stirring constantly and shaking the pan, until they are light golden brown, about 5 minutes. Transfer to a bowl and toss with paprika, salt, and pepper. Set aside.

Line two plates with paper towels. Put 3 cups of oil into a deep sauté pan fitted with a candy or deep-frying thermometer over medium heat until the temperature of the oil reaches 350°F. Add the kale and cook until crisp and the crackling stops, about 1 minute—be sure to keep an eye on it—as soon as it looks crisp remove it. Using a spider or slotted spoon, transfer the kale to a paper towel–lined plate to drain. Season with additional salt and pepper to taste.

Dust the onions with the flour and fry in the same oil you cooked the kale in, over medium heat, until golden brown, 2 to 3 minutes (but again, keep an eye on them! When they start to color, remove them). Remove the onions from the oil and transfer to a paper towel–lined plate to drain. Season with salt and pepper.

On a large serving platter, lay down the kale chips and the onions, then top with the spiced pine nuts and the grated cheese. Drizzle with lemon juice, and serve with lemon wedges (in case someone wants extra juice).

3 cups plus 1 tablespoon light olive oil (you can save this after)

⅔ cup pine nuts

1 teaspoon paprika

½ teaspoon kosher salt plus more as needed

½ teaspoon freshly ground black pepper plus more as needed

1 pound kale, ribs removed, leaves torn into 1½- to 2-inch pieces (use lacinato kale, also known as Tuscan or black kale if you can)

1 small onion, sliced into thin half-moons

2 tablespoons flour

½ cup grated pecorino Romano cheese

Juice of 1 lemon

Lemon wedges, for garnish

ON THE LIGHT SIDE

Soups, Salads, and Sandwiches

THERE ARE LOTS OF WAYS TO EAT WELL WITHOUT EATING HEAVILY.

Sandwiches are one kind of perfect light meal. Fill them with tasty lettuces, a light spread, and some deli cuts, and you've got a great, simple lunch to keep you fueled. Think about the bread as well as what goes on it—make it into an adventure. White and wheat are the easiest roads to take, but sometimes an olive loaf or maybe sun-dried tomato and oregano bread will take your sandwich to the next level.

If you're more in the mood for something really fresh, go for a salad. Bring on the fruits, the grains, the proteins, and the dressings! You are never limited as to what goes in your salad. How about tossing in candied walnuts with your arugula, and dressing it with a touch of aged balsamic and extra-virgin olive oil? Maybe some pomegranates and oranges with mixed greens and a lemon-basil dressing? My mouth is watering over here, people! The most important principle to remember is that the ingredients in a salad should not compete. You don't want flavors fighting each other, but rather, complementing one another. If you have a touch of spice, add a touch of sweet. Adding a touch of bitter or acidity at the end is a wonderful way to balance flavors.

The other category here is soups, a staple in my kitchen in all seasons. They're the perfect solution to our busy, hustle and bustle, "gotta-get-the-kids-to-school" kind of days. They can be hot or cold (there are recipes for both kinds here) and they don't require much attention once everything is in the pot, so you are able to step away from the stove for 30 minutes or 4 hours, depending on what you are making. Plus, the aroma just makes everything better. Studies show that releasing food aromas into your house actually can help reduce stress! Who doesn't like that? Soups can be simple, too. If you only have frozen peas, an onion, and beef stock, there is still hope for a great dinner. And a great dinner is the whole point no matter what you're eating, right?

Tomato Soup and Grilled Cheese

Classic on classic—this is just my spin on the grilled cheese. Use thicker crustier bread for a more challenging crunch.

MAKE THE SOUP: Melt the butter in a medium saucepan over medium-low heat. Add the onion and garlic and cook, stirring occasionally, until translucent, about 12 minutes.

Add the tomatoes and the stock and bring to a boil. Reduce the heat and simmer gently until thickened, about 45 minutes. Using an immersion blender, purée soup until smooth or, working in batches, purée the soup in a blender, starting on low and gradually increasing the speed. Be careful not to fill the blender more than halfway each time in order to leave space for air and to avoid a steam explosion.

Return the soup to a simmer over medium-low heat. Gradually add the cream, stirring constantly. Season with salt and pepper to taste. Garnish with a basil leaf, if desired. Serve hot.

MAKE THE SANDWICHES: Heat a griddle or large cast-iron skillet over medium-low heat. Cover 4 slices of the bread with a teaspoon each of mustard and Parmesan, and then a layer of cheese. Top with the remaining bread slices, pressing down with your hand (but don't overdo it). Butter both sides of each sandwich.

Cook two sandwiches at a time until the bread is golden brown and the cheese has melted, 4 to 5 minutes per side, turning once. Cut each sandwich diagonally in half and serve immediately with the soup.

Soup

2 tablespoons butter

1 red onion, finely chopped

4 garlic cloves, chopped

Three 28-ounce cans crushed tomatoes

5 cups chicken stock

½ cup heavy cream

Kosher salt and freshly ground black pepper

Fresh basil leaves (optional)

Sandwiches

Eight ½-inch-thick slices white sandwich bread

4 teaspoons Dijon mustard

¼ cup grated Parmesan cheese

½ pound cheddar or American cheese (if you are into really melty cheesy cheese, sliced ⅓ inch thick)

Butter, softened

Tomato Broth with Angel Hair Pasta

Light but satisfying, I love to make this in the late summer when tomatoes and herbs are at the height of their flavor.

While it doesn't bother me, I know some people prefer their tomatoes without skins for a sauce. To remove them easily, score an X with a knife on the very top of each tomato, drop them in boiling water for 30 seconds, and then transfer them immediately to ice water. Let them sit in the ice water for 3 minutes, then grab one corner of the X with your fingers and start peeling the skin off.

Preheat the oven to 450°F. Mix the cherry tomatoes with the regular olive oil and the salt, then spread them out on a sheet pan and roast them in the oven for 15 to 20 minutes, or until they start to get wrinkled and dry. Remove from the oven and set aside.

Put the regular tomatoes, garlic cloves, onion, and herb bundle in a tall stockpot, add the vegetable stock, and bring to a medium boil. Reduce the heat to very low, cover the pot, and simmer, stirring occasionally, for about 45 minutes, or until the tomatoes have completely melted in the stock. The liquid will have reduced by about one-third.

Let the broth cool for about 15 minutes, then remove and discard the thyme and basil bundle. Ladle the tomato mixture into a fine-mesh colander over a large bowl and use a mortar or the bottom of a ladle to push it through.

Clean the stockpot of any remains, return the clarified broth to it, and put it on the stovetop over high heat. Bring it to a boil. Break the angel hair pasta in half and drop it into the tomato broth. Remove the pot from the heat as soon as the pasta is cooked, about 5 minutes. Let the soup rest for about 2 minutes more, then serve hot with a drizzle of extra-virgin olive oil and a few of the roasted cherry tomatoes in each bowl for garnish.

½ pound small cherry tomatoes

2 tablespoons olive oil

½ teaspoon kosher salt

1 pound ripe tomatoes, halved

6 garlic cloves, peeled and cut in half

1 medium red onion, finely chopped

3 fresh thyme sprigs and 2 fresh basil stems tied together with butcher's twine

3½ cups vegetable stock

1 pound dried angel hair pasta

2 tablespoons extra-virgin olive oil

Brown Lentil and Pasta Soup with Parmesan Sour Cream

12 ounces dried brown lentils

2 fresh rosemary sprigs

8 slices pancetta, cut into small pieces

2 small red onions, chopped

3 garlic cloves, crushed

2 small carrots, peeled and diced

2 celery stalks, diced

3 to 4 cups vegetable stock

½ cup dried pasta for soup such as ditalini, rotini, or small farfalle

⅓ cup sour cream

2 tablespoons grated Parmesan cheese

For this recipe, you will need to start soaking the lentils with rosemary the night before. This helps flavor them and also shortens the cooking time because they will have absorbed water. Just think of it as a way to start building anticipation for the soup even earlier! This dish can also be done with split peas soaked the same way, which are easy to find at the store. You'll just need to taste as you go to adjust cooking time a bit.

The night before you will make the soup, put the lentils and the rosemary in a bowl and fill with water to cover the lentils. Let the lentils soak overnight.

Place the pancetta in a large, deep skillet over medium heat with the onions, garlic, carrot, and celery. Cook for 10 to 12 minutes, stirring, until the vegetables begin to caramelize.

Drain the lentils and add them, along with the stock, and bring to a boil. Reduce the heat to medium and cook until the lentils are done, about 30 minutes. They should be tender, but still a bit firm to the bite, like al dente pasta. If you see the broth reducing too much, cover the pan.

Drop the pasta in, cook for 5 minutes more and let rest for another 5. While it is resting, combine the sour cream and the Parmesan in a small bowl.

Serve the soup in bowls, garnished with a dollop of the Parmesan sour cream.

Chilled Corn Soup with Parmesan-Basil Corn Salad

12 ears sweet corn, shucked

1 large potato, peeled and diced (russet works best, but any kind will do)

2 bunches scallions, greens trimmed to 1 inch, and chopped

4 cups whole milk

2 cups half-and-half

1 jalapeño pepper, stems, seeds, and ribs removed, coarsely chopped

Kosher salt and freshly ground black pepper

½ cup sour cream (plus 1 teaspoon per person extra for garnish if you want)

20 fresh basil leaves

½ cup shaved Parmesan cheese

Extra-virgin olive oil

Perfect summer food, and perfect served in martini glasses for a festive gathering. You can make this in advance and refrigerate the soup for up to a week.

Cut the corn kernels off the cobs, set aside about 1 cup for adding later. Break each cob into two pieces. Put the cobs into a large pot along with the corn kernels, potatoes, scallions, milk, half-and-half, and jalapeños. Season with salt and black pepper.

Bring the mixture to a simmer over medium heat. Reduce the heat to low, cover, and simmer for 45 minutes.

Remove and discard the cobs. Add the sour cream. Using an immersion blender, purée soup until smooth or, working in batches, purée soup in a blender, starting on low and gradually increasing the speed. Be careful not to fill the blender more than halfway each time in order to leave space for air and to avoid a steam explosion. Strain it through a fine-mesh sieve into a bowl. Season with salt and pepper again.

Mix the basil, Parmesan, and 1 cup reserved corn kernels in a bowl. Drizzle with olive oil to taste and toss until all the ingredients are coated.

Cover and refrigerate the soup and the salad until cold, at least 1 hour. Serve the soup in chilled soup bowls with the salad as a garnish on top. If you like, you can add a small dollop of sour cream on top of the salad as well.

Chilled Potato and Pesto Soup

Many people like a potato chowder or a vichyssoise—this one adds my Italian exclamation point to it with a touch of pesto.

In a large saucepan, bring the leeks, potatoes, stock, water, cream, and salt to a boil. Reduce the heat to medium-low, and simmer until the vegetables are very tender, 20 to 25 minutes.

Using an immersion blender, purée the soup until smooth or, working in batches, purée the soup in a blender, starting on low and gradually increasing the speed. Be careful not to fill the blender more than halfway each time in order to leave space for air and to avoid a steam explosion.

Transfer the soup to a large bowl, cover with plastic wrap, and refrigerate until chilled, at least 2 hours. Before serving, thin the soup with water if necessary to achieve the desired consistency, and season with salt as needed. Serve the soup in chilled glasses, garnished with chives, croutons, and a dollop of pesto on top.

6 medium leeks, white parts only, well washed and sliced in ¼-inch rounds

2 pounds russet potatoes, peeled and diced

4 cups chicken stock

2 cups water

1 cup heavy cream

2 teaspoons kosher salt, plus additional as needed

½ cup snipped fresh chives, for garnish

As many croutons as you like (homemade if you want to!)

1 cup fresh pesto (recipe below)

Pesto

Combine the basil, spinach, garlic, pine nuts, salt, pepper, and Parmesan in a food processor and pulse to partially combine. Turn the processor on Auto and drizzle in the olive oil, a half cup at a time, until the ingredients start to come together into a chunky paste. Make sure to add the oil a little at a time to ensure a non-runny pesto.

3 cups packed fresh basil leaves

1 cup baby spinach

4 garlic cloves, chopped

⅓ cup pine nuts

Kosher salt and freshly ground black pepper

½ cup grated Parmesan cheese

½ to 1½ cups extra-virgin olive oil, depending on your desired thickness

Mussel Soup with Dark Beer

3 tablespoons extra-virgin
  olive oil

2 small white onions, finely
  chopped

2 celery stalks, finely chopped

4 garlic cloves, crushed

2 teaspoons fresh marjoram
  leaves

Freshly ground black pepper

16 ounces crushed canned
  tomatoes

1½ cups dark or amber beer

Kosher salt

3 pounds mussels, cleaned and
  de-bearded

¼ cup heavy cream

Some Garlic Crostini (page 15)

½ cup chopped fresh flat-leaf
  parsley

For a more "adult" dish, try adding a touch of Pernod to the soup at the very end. A shot glass is just the right amount, and the extra layer of flavor will make a big difference.

Heat the olive oil in a deep, wide sauté pan over medium heat, add the onions, and sauté. As soon as the onions begin to caramelize, add the celery, garlic, marjoram, and pepper to taste.

When the celery and garlic have started to caramelize, add the tomatoes and let them stew for 3 to 4 minutes. Add the beer and season to taste with kosher salt. Bring to a slow boil and let the mixture bubble for 5 minutes before covering it and turning down the flame. Cook until the tomatoes are almost reduced to pulp, 6 to 8 minutes. Add the mussels.

Cook for about 5 minutes, then add the cream. Cook for another 5 minutes or so until all the mussels have opened. Remove from heat and discard any mussels that did not open.

Place as many garlic crostini as you like at the bottom of each of four bowls, then spoon the mussels and sauce over the crostini for serving. Garnish with some chopped parsley. Don't forget to put a large bowl on the table for empty shells!

Fast Red Bouillabaisse (Fish Soup)

SERVES 4

Look, I understand that real-long-time-on-the-stove kind of thing. Authentic bouillabaisse is tasty, but sometimes you just don't have the time or you don't feel like making the effort. This recipe is not only really good it's almost as good as the real thing. For a quick meal, it's the next big thing.

MAKE THE TOASTS: Preheat the oven to 350°F. Combine the mayonnaise with the garlic, parsley, and chives. Set aside.

Cut the baguette into thin slices and arrange on a baking sheet. Toast in the oven until they are nice and crunchy and golden brown, 5 to 8 minutes. Set aside.

MAKE THE SOUP: Heat the olive oil in a medium saucepan over medium heat, add the onion, garlic, and fennel and cook until soft and brown. Add the tomato purée, reserved clam juice, and saffron and raise the heat to high. Keep stirring until the tomato purée starts to reduce and most of the water has evaporated, 5 to 6 minutes. Add the fish stock and cream, turn the heat down to low, and simmer for about 15 minutes. Add the fish, mussels, clams, and shrimp and continue simmering until they are cooked, another 6 to 7 minutes.

To serve, divide the fish, mussels, and shrimp evenly among four bowls, then cover with the broth. Spread each toast with some of the herb mayonnaise and serve alongside the soup.

Toasts

6 tablespoons good-quality mayonnaise

2 garlic cloves, finely minced

2 tablespoons finely chopped fresh flat-leaf parsley

2 tablespoons finely chopped fresh chives

1 baguette

Soup

3 tablespoons extra-virgin olive oil

1 red onion, diced

3 garlic cloves, crushed

1 fennel bulb, cleaned, trimmed, and finely sliced

One 8-ounce can tomato purée

1 teaspoon saffron

3 cups fish stock

⅓ cup heavy cream

One 15-ounce can clams, drained, juices reserved

Juice from the drained clams, plus additional clam juice or fish stock to make 1 cup

2 pounds fish fillets, diced (any thick fillets of firm-fleshed white fish such as cod, halibut, or snapper will do)

15 mussels, cleaned

16 medium clams, cleaned

20 medium shrimp, peeled and
   deveined, tails left on

Chicken and Dumplings

Chicken Stew

2 tablespoons light olive oil

2 pounds boneless, skinless chicken thighs (5 to 6 thighs)

Kosher salt and freshly ground black pepper

1 tablespoon butter

2 small white onions, finely chopped

3 cups chicken stock (home-made if you have it)

2 teaspoons fresh thyme leaves

3 tablespoons cornstarch

1 cup half-and-half

Pinch of salt, for blanching

1 teaspoon baking soda

1 tablespoon sugar

3 carrots, peeled and cut into ¼-inch-thick spears

10 ounces fresh or frozen green peas

I love this dish and eat it whenever I can. The dumplings here are made out of polenta and they are precious. If you can, make extra dumplings and bake them with a sprinkle of Parmesan on top.

MAKE THE CHICKEN STEW: Heat the olive oil in a Dutch oven or large deep skillet over medium heat. Add the chicken, season with salt and pepper, and cook for 8 to 10 minutes, turning once, until browned and cooked through. Remove the thighs from the pot and set them aside to cool.

Using the same pot, cook the onions in the butter for about 10 minutes. Add the chicken stock and the thyme, bring to a boil, and reduce by one-third. While it is reducing, shred the cooled chicken meat.

Put the cornstarch in a bowl and gradually whisk in the half-and-half. When it is fully combined, then whisk the mixture into the pot of chicken stock. Keep whisking and cooking, until thickened, about 10 minutes. Add the shredded chicken to the pot and stir to combine. Remove from heat.

Bring a medium saucepan of water to a boil and add salt, baking soda, and sugar. Blanch the carrots and peas in the water until cooked but still crisp, about 5 minutes. Drain in a colander, and then rinse with cold water to stop the cooking. Add them into the chicken mixture.

— {Continued} —

MAKE THE DUMPLINGS: Whisk together the flour, grated cheese, garlic powder, cornmeal, baking powder, and salt. Work the butter into the flour mixture with a fork until it is the texture of coarse meal. Pour in the half-and-half and combine with the fork until the dough just comes together.

Return the chicken mixture to a simmer over low heat, then drop the dough by tablespoons on top. Cover and cook 15 minutes without lifting the lid. Serve hot.

Dumplings

1 cup flour

2 tablespoons grated Parmesan cheese

2 teaspoons garlic powder

½ cup yellow cornmeal

3 teaspoons baking powder

½ teaspoon kosher salt

2 tablespoons cold butter, cut into small pieces

1 cup half-and-half

Shrimp and Chicken Andouille Gumbo from My Louisiana Roommate's Mom

SERVES 8

To make a tasty rice to serve with this gumbo, cook it with chicken stock in a Dutch oven. Start with ½ cup rice and 1 cup stock per person, cooking and stirring until the stock is absorbed. Then cover the rice with stock again (about ½ cup stock for each ½ cup rice), cover the pan, and turn the heat down to low. Cook it until all the liquid is gone, stirring once in a while to make sure the rice is not sticking to the bottom of the pan.

Preheat the oven to 375°F. Toss the chicken thighs with the 2 tablespoons of olive oil, season with salt and black pepper to taste and put them in a baking pan. Roast in the oven for about 30 minutes, or until the juices run clear when the thighs are pierced with the tip of a small knife. You can proceed with the recipe while the thighs cook—just remember to set a timer!

Put the sausage in a large, heavy pot or Dutch oven over medium heat and cook for about 10 minutes. Remove from heat. Using a slotted spoon, transfer the sausage to a plate. Add the ½ cup oil to the pot and gradually sprinkle in the flour, stirring until it is incorporated. Cook over medium-low heat, stirring often, until the roux is a deep brown color, about 45 minutes to 1 hour. If the roux begins to smoke, remove the pot from the heat for a few minutes, and then resume cooking over lower heat.

Add the celery, onion, bell pepper, and garlic to the pot. Raise the heat to medium-high and cook, stirring frequently, reducing the heat if roux is smoking, until the vegetables have softened, 5 to 8 minutes. Add the thyme and bay leaves, season with salt, and keep cooking for 5 minutes more.

6 bone-in chicken thighs (about 2½ pounds), skin removed

½ cup plus 2 tablespoons light olive oil

Kosher salt and freshly ground black pepper

1½ pounds andouille sausage, sliced into ¼-inch rounds

1 cup flour

3 celery stalks, cut into ½-inch dice

1 medium onion, cut into ½-inch dice

1 red bell pepper, seeds and membranes removed, cut into ½-inch dice

6 garlic cloves, finely chopped

1 teaspoon dried thyme

2 dried bay leaves

6 cups chicken stock

16 ounces crushed canned tomatoes

2 tablespoons filé powder (optional)

30 medium shrimp, peeled, tail on, deveined if you like

— {Continued} —

Gradually stir the stock into the vegetable mixture, stirring and scraping the bottom of the pot until everything is thoroughly combined. Stir in the tomatoes and their juice, and add the chicken. Raise the heat to medium and bring to a boil. Add the andouille, and the filé powder if using. Reduce the heat to a steady simmer and cook, stirring occasionally, until the sauce has thickened, about 45 minutes. Add the shrimp, remove the pot from the heat, cover it, and let the shrimp cook in the sauce for another 15 minutes. Then bring the pot to a boil and immediately remove it from the fire.

Remove the bay leaves from the pot and discard. Serve the gumbo hot over boiled rice if you want.

Chunky Sausage and Clam Chowder

Classic chowder move over! The Italians are coming and they are chasing you with some really tasty sausages!

In a large heavy-bottomed pot over medium heat, melt the butter. Add the sausage and cook until the sausage is golden brown. Remove the sausage from the pot and set aside on a plate. Add the red onions, thyme, and bay leaves and sauté in the fat until the onions are caramel-colored. Add the potatoes and cook for 5 minutes more.

Pour in the clam juice, then add the corn, and simmer for about 10 minutes. Season the chowder well with salt and pepper and stir, making sure to break up some of the potatoes. Cook for another 10 to 12 minutes over medium heat, until the liquid has reduced by at least one-third. Return the sausage to the pot and add the clams. Stir in the cream and taste for salt and pepper. Add additional if needed. Remove from heat and let the chowder stand for at least 1 hour. Reheat the soup over medium heat; do not let it boil. Just before eating, sprinkle with parsley and chives. Serve with crusty bread.

2 tablespoons butter

12 ounces sweet or hot Italian sausage, casings removed

2 red onions, diced

1 tablespoon fresh thyme leaves

2 bay leaves

4 medium russet potatoes, peeled and diced

Clam juice from two 15-ounce cans clams, plus enough additional clam juice or fish stock to make 4 cups

½ cup fresh corn kernels, or drained canned corn, or thawed frozen kernels

Kosher salt and freshly ground black pepper

Two 15-ounce cans clams, drained, juices reserved

1 cup heavy cream

1 bunch fresh flat-leaf parsley, washed, stemmed, and chopped

1 bunch fresh chives, chopped

Oxtail Soup with Barley and Mushrooms

3 pounds oxtails, cut into
  2-inch chunks (ask your
  butcher to do this for you)
Kosher salt and freshly ground
  black pepper
¼ cup flour
¼ cup light olive oil, plus more
  as needed
2 large red onions, roughly
  chopped
2 celery stalks, roughly
  chopped
2 medium carrots, peeled and
  chopped into ½-inch rounds
3 garlic cloves, minced
3 cups finely sliced fresh oyster
  mushrooms
2 tablespoons porcini mushroom powder (optional—fine
  to omit if you don't have it)
1 quart beef stock or water
  (you may not use it all)
4 fresh thyme sprigs, or 1 teaspoon dried thyme
1 bay leaf
⅔ cup barley
Chopped fresh flat-leaf parsley,
  for garnish
½ cup grated pecorino
  Romano cheese

B raising makes me relaxed and the earthiness of this dish is pure comfort. Got a pillow anyone?

Season the oxtails with salt and pepper to taste. Place the flour in a plastic bag, put in the oxtails, and seal it. Shake to coat the oxtails.

Heat 2 tablespoons of the oil in a large soup pot over medium-high heat. Working in batches, add the oxtails and cook, turning occasionally, until browned, about 10 minutes for each piece. Transfer the oxtails to a plate.

Heat the remaining 2 tablespoons oil in the same pot over medium heat. (Don't worry about the brown bits, that's called flavor!) Add the onion, celery, carrots, and garlic and cook until the vegetables caramelize, about 20 minutes. Add the sliced mushrooms and the porcini powder, if using, and cook until they are wilted, about 5 minutes.

Return the oxtails to the pot. Add enough broth to just cover the meat and vegetables, reserving the rest to add later in case your sauce reduces too much. Bring to a boil over high heat and add the thyme and bay leaf. Reduce the heat to medium-low and simmer, partially covered, for 2 hours. Add the barley and continue cooking until the meat and barley are tender, about 1 hour more, adding more of the reserved broth if needed.

Remove the pot from the heat and let stand 15 minutes, uncovered. Skim off any fat that rises to the surface. Season to taste with salt and pepper.

Ladle into soup bowls and sprinkle each serving with parsley and some pecorino cheese.

Fresh Tuna Salad Sandwiches

3 garlic cloves, crushed

5 bay leaves

Whole black peppercorns,
   to taste

3 cups water

1 pound tuna fillets, cut into 4
   pieces

1 cup good-quality mayon-
   naise

2 teaspoons Dijon mustard

½ cup diced celery

2 teaspoons finely grated
   lemon zest

2 teaspoons fresh lemon juice

Kosher salt and freshly ground
   black pepper

½ small red onion, diced

½ cup fresh flat-leaf parsley
   leaves

2 tablespoons capers

2 hard-boiled eggs, chopped

2 baguettes cut in half, then
   split lengthwise

I t's time that America learned how not to use canned tuna. Making your own is not only easy but a thousand times tastier.

Put the garlic, bay leaves, and peppercorn in a pot big enough to hold all the tuna along with the water. Heat almost to boiling, then put the tuna into the water, lower the heat, and simmer for about 10 minutes. Remove the fish from water, pat dry, transfer to a plate and place it in the fridge to cool down.

Combine the mayonnaise, mustard, celery, lemon zest, lemon juice, salt, pepper, onion, parsley, capers, and eggs together in a large bowl. Add the cooled tuna and mix well, breaking the fish up with a fork.

Spread the tuna salad onto the bottom side of the baguette halves and top with the other piece. Cut each sandwich in half and serve.

Louisville Hot Brown Turkey Sandwich

MAKES 8 OPEN-FACED SANDWICHES

The best turkey for this is whatever is left over from Thanksgiving, finely shredded. (The Hot Brown Sandwich is a classic at my better half's house the day after Thanksgiving—not that she cooks anything, but she definitely knows how to shred some turkey!) If you crave this in June or February, just grab some turkey breast slices.

Put the butter, flour, and pepper in a medium pot over low heat and cook, stirring to combine, until the butter has melted. Add the milk and stir until creamy and thick. Remove from heat.

In a heatproof bowl, beat the egg yolks with the hot sauce.

Gradually stir the hot mixture into the bowl of beaten egg yolks, whisking fast as you add it. When it is all combined, return the mixture to the pot. Cook over low heat, stirring, until the sauce just starts to bubble again. Remove from heat and stir in ⅓ cup of the grated cheese.

Toast the bread in a toaster or in the oven at 375°F until it starts to brown.

Arrange the slices of toast in a single layer on a broiler pan. Top each piece with 3 slices of turkey (keep it in a heap, don't press them down!), 1 to 2 spoonfuls of sauce, and some Parmesan cheese. (Make sure you save a little bit of the cheese for garnish.)

Turn on the broiler and broil the sandwiches 4 to 5 inches from the heat for 3 to 5 minutes, or until the sauce is bubbly. To serve, top each sandwich with two slices of cooked bacon and two slices of tomato.

5 tablespoons (½ stick plus 1 tablespoon) butter, at room temperature

2½ tablespoons flour

1 teaspoon freshly ground black pepper

2⅓ cups milk

2 egg yolks, slightly beaten

1 tablespoon hot sauce

⅔ cup grated Parmesan cheese

8 slices white bread

24 thin slices roasted turkey

16 strips fully cooked smoked bacon

16 thin tomato slices

Roasted Vegetable Panini

1 bell pepper, any color, stemmed, cored, and seeded, and cut lengthwise in half

1 zucchini, sliced into ½-inch-thick spears, ends discarded

1 eggplant, peeled and sliced into ½-inch rounds, ends discarded

¼ cup extra-virgin olive oil

1 teaspoon garlic powder

2 garlic cloves, crushed

1 shallot, roughly chopped

1 tablespoon chopped fresh flat-leaf parsley

1 demi baguette

1 tablespoon Dijon mustard

4 teaspoons grated Parmesan cheese

2 tablespoons chopped scallions

4 slices Fontina cheese

Packed with flavor and texture, this is far away from your usual "please don't do it!" veggie burger.

Preheat the oven to 400°F.

Combine the bell peppers, zucchini, and eggplant in a large bowl.

In a smaller bowl, mix the olive oil, garlic powder, garlic, shallot, and parsley until they are well combined. Add the dressing to the bowl of veggies and toss until they are all well coated.

Transfer the vegetables to a rimmed baking sheet in one layer and roast in the oven for 15 to 20 minutes, or until the eggplant starts to brown and the pepper starts to soften. Take the veggies out and start to build the sandwich.

Cut the baguette in half, then slice each piece lengthwise to make two bottoms and two tops. Spread ½ tablespoon of the mustard on each bottom half, dust with 2 teaspoons of the grated Parmesan on each half, then top each with 1 tablespoon of scallions.

Layer on the roasted vegetables, starting with the eggplant, then adding the zucchini, and finally the bell peppers. Place 2 slices of Fontina on each sandwich, then the top half of each roll, and bake for about 5 minutes.

Philly Cheesesteak

This is my favorite sandwich of all time. It combines the best of three worlds: melting cheese, thin-sliced steak, and a beautiful hoagie roll. I was introduced to this by the king of Philly cheesesteaks, Tony Luke.

¼ cup extra-light olive oil

1 large onion, diced

1 pound rib eye steak, well marbled and sliced as thinly as possible (ask your butcher!)

¼ pound provolone cheese, thinly sliced

2 hoagie or other rolls, about 8 inches long

Heat the olive oil in a flat griddle pan over very high heat. Add the onion to the griddle, cook for a few minutes until nicely browned. Transfer to a plate and keep warm.

Put the sliced steak onto the griddle and cook, turning it, for a few minutes, just until the pink disappears. Just before the meat finishes cooking, spread it out to about the length of your rolls, then lay the slices of cheese over the meat so they can melt a little bit.

Slice the rolls open lengthwise, and place them, upside down, over the meat, building a tent. Using the bread, scoop half of the meat and cheese off of the griddle into each. *Be careful.*

Top with the grilled onions. Slice and serve.

Tomato Tart

1 package store-bought puff
    pastry sheets

About 1 pound fresh tomatoes,
    seeded and cut into ¼ inch-
    thick slices

1 tablespoon chopped fresh
    thyme

1 tablespoon chopped fresh
    rosemary

Kosher salt and freshly ground
    black pepper

2 garlic cloves, crushed

2 tablespoons extra-virgin
    olive oil

10 to 15 fresh basil leaves

¼ cup grated Parmesan cheese

I normally make this when tomato season starts in California; it can be made with sweet ripe tomatoes or with green ones for more of a tart flavor. The tart can be eaten cold or hot.

Preheat the oven to 375°F. Line a rimmed cookie sheet or half sheet pan with a piece of parchment paper.

Lay the dough onto the paper and poke it with the tines of a fork across the whole surface. Bake the dough for 10 minutes and remove it from the oven.

Lay the tomato slices over the dough so they overlap slightly. Distribute the thyme, rosemary, salt, and pepper evenly over the tomatoes, scatter the pieces of garlic on top, and drizzle with the olive oil.

Bake the tart for another 25 to 30 minutes, or until the pastry starts to turn dark golden on the outside. Remove the tart from the oven, scatter the basil leaves and Parmesan on top, and serve.

Leek and Brie Pie

Sometimes leeks aren't available (they're best in late summer). But this dish is delicious any time of year, so if you don't have leeks, you can replace them with the same amount of shallots and scallions combined. For a non-vegetarian version, add a cup of diced, smoked ham.

Preheat the oven to 400°F. Line a half sheet pan with parchment paper.

Stack the puff pastry sheets and roll them out lengthwise to fit your pan; make sure the dough is not less than ¼ inch thick. Using the back of a knife, score a rectangle about 1 inch wide around the inside of the pastry edge, like a picture frame. Carefully transfer the puff pastry to the prepared pan. Work as quickly as you can with the dough so that it doesn't get too warm and start to disintegrate.

Place the butter, leeks, white wine, thyme, salt, and pepper in a saucepan and simmer over high heat for about 20 minutes, or until all the liquid has evaporated.

Spread the leeks inside the scored lines of the puff pastry. Top with the cheese and brush the outer edges of the pastry with the egg white.

Bake for 25 minutes; the edges will rise considerably. If you find the pastry is getting too brown at any point, cover it loosely with aluminum foil for the remainder of the baking time. Place the pie on a serving platter and cut into squares.

1 package store-bought puff pastry sheets
4 tablespoons (½ stick) butter
5 cups well washed and thinly sliced leeks, white parts only
¾ cup dry white wine
2 teaspoons fresh thyme leaves
Kosher salt and freshly ground black pepper
10 ounces Brie or Cambozola cheese, cut into little pieces
1 egg white, lightly beaten

Chicago-Style "Homemade Deep-Dish Pizza"

MAKES 1 PIZZA; ABOUT 8 SLICES

Now that I have restaurants in Chicago, I often find myself going home and stuffing my face with deep-dish pizza. It's delicious, and then I feel bad about myself and run 5 miles. If you like a less watery texture for the sauce cook the tomatoes for an extra 15 minutes or so until all the water has reduced.

MAKE THE SAUCE: In a deep saucepan over medium heat, combine tomatoes, garlic, fennel seeds, red pepper flakes, sugar, basil, thyme, oregano, red wine, and olive oil. Stir to combine.

Bring the sauce to a boil, lower heat to a simmer, and allow to reduce for 20 to 30 minutes, until thickened.

Season with salt and black pepper to taste. Set the sauce aside and allow it to cool completely before assembling the pizza.

ASSEMBLE THE PIZZA: Preheat the oven to 475°F. Oil the bottom and sides of a 9-inch round cake pan.

On a floured work surface, stretch the dough to an even thickness, so it's large enough to cover the entire interior surface of the pan, including the sides. Allow the dough to rest for 5 minutes before building the pizza.

Cover the dough with mozzarella, and top with cooked Italian sausage. Top with the green bell pepper rings, sliced mushrooms, and onion rings. Layer the pepperoni evenly over the vegetables. Ladle sauce over the pepperoni to cover, then top with an even layer of grated Parmesan. Brush the visible edges of the crust with extra-virgin olive oil.

Bake the pizza for 30 to 35 minutes until golden brown. Remove from the oven, slice, and serve hot.

Dough

½ batch of Fabio's Pizza Dough (about 1 pound of dough) (page 65), or any other frozen or fresh pizza dough

Flour, for dusting

Sauce

16 ounces canned crushed plum tomatoes

1 tablespoon chopped garlic

⅛ teaspoon fennel seeds

⅛ teaspoon crushed red pepper flakes

½ teaspoon sugar

1 teaspoon dried basil

½ teaspoon dried thyme

½ teaspoon dried oregano

1 tablespoon dry red wine

½ tablespoon extra-virgin olive oil

Kosher salt and freshly ground black pepper

Toppings

One 8-ounce part-skim mozzarella cheese ball, sliced or crumbled

¼ pound hot Italian sausage, casings removed, fully

cooked and crumbled
(1 or 2 sausages)

½ green bell pepper, cored,
seeded, and cut into thin
rings

¾ cup thinly sliced oyster
mushrooms

¼ yellow onion, cut into thin
rings

2 ounces pepperoni, thinly
sliced

½ cup grated Parmesan cheese

Extra-virgin olive oil

Fabio's Pizza Dough

1 packet (or ¼ ounce) active
dry yeast

1½ cups warm water

1 teaspoon sugar

4 cups flour, plus a few pinches
for dusting

1 tablespoon extra-virgin
olive oil

In a stand mixer fitted with the hook attachment, mix the yeast, water, and sugar. Add the flour in small amounts, mixing well between each addition until it is all incorporated.

When the dough is mixed well and not too sticky, use a little oil to help remove it from the bowl. Place the dough on a lightly floured work surface, cover it with a dry linen towel, and let it rise for 30 minutes.

Spicy Sausage Pasta Salad   SERVES 6

Two Italian staples are combined here so we can enjoy a little pasta on a hot summer day. Because we are Italian and we eat pasta. Always. Got it?

Bring a large pot of lightly salted water (the sausages in the dish are plenty salty, so you don't want to overdo it!) to a boil over medium heat. Add the pasta and cook for 6 minutes; it will be very al dente. Drain and set aside.

Heat the oil in a deep sauté pan over medium heat. Add the onion and cook until translucent, then stir in the garlic, bell peppers, and sausage and cook for 10 to 12 minutes until the sausage is fully cooked. If you are using sausage that is already cooked, shorten your cooking time by about 5 minutes so the veggies are cooked and the sausage is heated through.

Add the wine and reserved pasta to the pan, stir, and bring the mixture just to a boil over medium heat. Cook until the liquid has reduced completely. Let cool for 10 minutes on the countertop, then put it in the fridge for another 30 minutes.

Combine the mayonnaise, grated cheese, mustard, basil, chiles, salt, and black pepper in a large bowl, then mix in the pasta and sausage. To serve, place the salad greens on a large platter and spoon the pasta mixture on top of them.

8 ounces dried orecchiette

2 tablespoons extra-virgin olive oil

1 medium red onion, diced

1 garlic clove, smashed

1 cup diced mixed bell peppers (red, green, yellow)

1 pound spicy pork sausage, such as salami or chorizo, or cooked Italian sausage, sliced into thin rounds

⅓ cup red wine

¼ cup mayonnaise

2 tablespoons grated pecorino Romano cheese

2 tablespoons Dijon mustard

30 fresh basil leaves, torn into pieces

2 hot red peppers (like red jalapeños), thinly sliced

Kosher salt and freshly ground black pepper

¾ pound mixed salad greens

Rare Beef Pasta Salad

1 pound skirt steak (all in 1
  piece)
Kosher salt and freshly ground
  black pepper
1 pound dried pasta (orecchiette, fusilli, or mezzi
  rigatoni)
¼ cup extra-virgin olive oil
2 tablespoons fresh lemon
  juice
2 tablespoons balsamic vinegar
2 teaspoons molasses
1 tablespoon Dijon mustard
⅓ cup pitted sliced olives
3 different colored tomatoes,
  heirloom varieties if you
  can find them, cut into
  wedges
30 fresh basil leaves
1 pound mixed salad greens
2 bunches green scallions, ends
  trimmed, thinly sliced
½ cup grated Parmesan cheese

Who says summer is too hot for grilling or for a good piece of meat? I'd eat salad every day if it came with a side of steak. Use skirt steak for more flavor, or filet mignon for super tender texture. (If you choose filet, cook it on the grill until its internal temperature reaches 140°F.) The secret to getting the best from either cut is slicing it thin.

Season the steak with salt and pepper. In a cast-iron pan over medium heat, sear the meat for about 3 minutes each side, then remove and set aside for 5 minutes before slicing thinly against the grain.

Meanwhile, bring a large pot of salted water to a boil over medium heat. Add the pasta and cook for 8 minutes (it will be al dente). Drain the pasta and run it under cold water, let it sit for 5 minutes, then combine it with the oil in a bowl.

Mix the lemon juice, vinegar, molasses, and mustard together in a small saucepan and cook over medium heat for about 2 minutes. Remove from the heat and, once it has cooled down, add it with the olives and tomatoes to the skillet and stir to combine. Add the steak and mix again. Season with salt and pepper to taste, then add the contents of the skillet to the bowl containing the pasta and olive oil with the torn basil leaves, and combine well.

Pile the greens in the bottom of a large bowl, then spoon the pasta salad on top of them. Sprinkle with the scallions and Parmesan and serve.

Pasta Salad with Walnuts, Gorgonzola, and Mozzarella

SERVES 4

Here's an Italian pasta salad that doesn't feature meat. You can use different cheeses and nuts as well—try cashews, pecans, or peanuts.

Preheat the oven to 350°F. Place half of the walnuts in a roasting pan and toast in the oven for 20 minutes, then set aside to cool.

While the nuts are toasting, bring a large pot of salted water to a boil. Add the pasta, return to a boil, and cook for 8 minutes. Drain and run under cold water.

In a large bowl, combine the vinegar, salad greens, Gorgonzola, kale, Parmesan, mozzarella, and parsley. Add the pasta and both the toasted and untoasted nuts, and mix gently. Drizzle with the olive oil and season with salt and pepper to taste.

1 cup chopped or crushed walnuts

10 ounces fusilli

2 tablespoons balsamic vinegar

¾ pound mixed salad greens

8 ounces Gorgonzola cheese, diced or crumbled

2 cups finely chopped kale

⅓ cup grated Parmesan cheese

6 ounces mozzarella cheese, diced

1 cup whole flat-leaf parsley leaves

2 tablespoons extra-virgin olive oil

Kosher salt and freshly ground black pepper

Grilled Shrimp on Arugula with Lemon Vinaigrette

1 pound medium shrimp,
    peeled and deveined if you
    like
Kosher salt and freshly ground
    black pepper
1 cup plus 1 tablespoon
    extra-virgin olive oil
Finely grated zest of 1 lemon
¼ cup fresh lemon juice
1 tablespoon honey
1 tablespoon Dijon mustard
1 tablespoon white balsamic
    vinegar
3 cups baby arugula, well
    washed

This dish is healthy, nutritious, and packed with flavors. If you're serving it right away, when the shrimp is just off the grill, lime juice will work magic. For a more pungent flavor, you can try drizzling the shrimp with a touch of balsamic vinegar.

You can cook the shrimp with or without their shells, as you prefer.

Preheat the grill to medium-high heat.

Toss the shrimp with salt, pepper, and 1 tablespoon of the olive oil in a large bowl.

Once the grill is heated, place the shrimp on the grill and cook for 1 to 1½ minutes. Flip, then cook about the same amount of time on the other side for a total of 2 to 3 minutes. Remove the shrimp from the grill and keep warm.

Combine the remaining 1 cup olive oil and the lemon zest, lemon juice, honey, mustard, and white balsamic in a blender and blend together well. Toss the shrimp with 1 teaspoon of the dressing to start, then add more until you have achieved the flavor you want. Do the same with the arugula. Serve the shrimp and arugula side by side and enjoy!

GREAT GRAIN

Pasta and Rice

NATIONS HAVE BEEN USING PASTA AND GRAINS FOR CURRENCY and consumption for hundreds of years, and my feeling is, if it's not broke, don't fix it. Actually, even if you break pasta, it's still good!

In America, dried pasta is the style of choice and the most used shapes are penne, spaghetti, and lasagna sheets. For what reason these have become the favorite, I'm not sure. I cook food; I don't take opinion surveys. No matter what shape it is, though, pasta is a great choice for a meal, hot or cold. I prefer mine served with Pomodoro (fresh tomato sauce) or with black pepper and Parmesan. And always al dente. *Always.* Al dente means "to the tooth," or in common talk, "it has bite." That slight crunch gives the pasta texture and something to sink your teeth into. I only allow pasta to be "overcooked" in two dishes—lasagna and pasta salad. Both are delicious, and both can be made in large amounts for families or parties. Other than these two options, please do not overcook my pasta.

Various companies are getting creative these days with tri-color, spinach, and tomato varieties of pasta. The demand for gluten-free products in America has resulted in corn, rice, and quinoa pastas. Looking for more whole grains? Choose a whole wheat pasta. This type will need a couple more minutes to cook, but will give you great results. If you can boil water, you can make pasta. If you can read, you can make pasta. But if for some reason you still think you can't, I'm so passionate about pasta that I will show up at your house, heat the water, cook the pasta, and make sure that your palette goes to a heavenly place.

Risotto from the Oven with Sausage and Bell Pepper

This is the reason why Italy is so awesome. Americans complain about all the stirring needed to make risotto? Now the oven does the job for you!

Preheat the oven to 350°F.

Heat the oil over medium-high heat in a heavy Dutch oven. Crumble the sausage meat and salami over the hot oil in the pot. Turn over a few times with a wooden spoon.

Add the bell peppers, onions, garlic, thyme, and fennel seeds and cook until the vegetables are browned, 12 to 15 minutes. Add the tomato sauce and keep cooking, stirring continuously, over high heat for another 5 minutes.

Add in the rice and cook for another minute. Add the wine and stir in the stock, then bring the mixture to a boil while stirring. Cover the pot with a lid and place in the oven. Bake for 30 to 40 minutes, or until all the liquid is absorbed. Stir in the Parmesan and serve.

- 2 tablespoons extra-virgin olive oil
- 1 pound sweet Italian sausage, casings removed
- 4 ounces salami, casing removed and finely diced
- 2 red bell peppers, ribs and seeds removed, cut into small dice
- 2 yellow bell peppers, ribs and seeds removed, cut into small dice
- 2 small red onions, finely chopped
- 3 garlic cloves, slivered
- 2 teaspoons fresh thyme leaves, chopped
- 2 teaspoons fennel seeds
- 1½ cups Fabio's Tomato Sauce (below)
- 1½ cups Arborio rice
- 1½ cups dry red wine
- 1½ cups chicken stock
- ½ cup grated Parmesan cheese

Fabio's Tomato Sauce

MAKES 3 CUPS SAUCE

Smash the garlic with the back of a knife. Place the garlic and 5 tablespoons (⅓ cup) of the olive oil in a saucepan and cook over

- 6 garlic cloves
- ½ cup extra-virgin olive oil

One 28-ounce can whole plum
    tomatoes
Kosher salt and freshly ground
    black pepper
10 fresh basil leaves, torn

medium heat until the garlic is golden brown. Add the tomatoes and
generous pinches of salt and pepper.

Cook over medium-high heat until the sauce is thick and no
longer watery, 10 to 15 minutes. Add the remaining 3 tablespoons
olive oil and increase the heat to high. Stir, crushing the tomatoes
with the back of a wooden spoon, and cook until the oil turns red,
then turn off the heat and add the basil at the very end.

Red Beans and Rice

We used to eat bone-in ham on certain Sundays when I was growing up, and I learned that saving the bone for the next day's soup or to add to broth used for cooking beans adds a tremendous amount of flavor. If you have one hanging around, this is the perfect use for it. Also, feel free to adjust the amounts of chili powder and Tabasco to make the recipe less or more spicy. And remember, the beans need to soak overnight, so plan ahead!

2 pounds dried red beans, picked over and rinsed

5 fresh bay leaves

1 pound spicy Italian sausage, casings removed

5 tablespoons (½ stick plus 1 tablespoon) butter

6 garlic cloves, finely chopped

6 celery stalks, finely chopped

2 onions, chopped

2 red bell peppers, ribs and seeds removed, finely chopped

2 tablespoons chili powder

1 tablespoon smoked paprika

3 tablespoons Tabasco sauce

Kosher salt and freshly ground black pepper

Chopped fresh flat-leaf parsley, for garnish (optional)

4 to 5 cups cooked white rice (about ½ cup per person)

Combine the beans and bay leaves in a bowl of cold water and leave overnight to soak.

Preheat the oven to 375°F. Crumble the Italian sausage into a pan and bake it until it is cooked through, 10 to 12 minutes.

Melt the butter in a Dutch oven over medium heat. Add the sausage and garlic and cook until the garlic is golden brown, stirring frequently, 1 to 2 minutes. Add the celery, onions, bell peppers, chili powder, and paprika. Cook, stirring occasionally, until the vegetables have softened, about 10 minutes.

Drain the beans and bay leaves and add them to the pot, along with the Tabasco, salt and pepper to taste, and enough water to cover the beans. Bring to a boil, reduce to a simmer, and cook, uncovered, until the beans are tender, about 1½ hours. Remove and discard the bay leaves. Add parsley, if using, and stir to combine. Serve immediately over the cooked rice.

NOTE: To make "dirty rice" toss some of the cooked white rice with the cooking liquid from the beans.

Spaghetti Olio e Aglio with Peperoncini

1 pound spaghetti

½ cup extra-virgin olive oil

8 garlic cloves, finely chopped

3 tablespoons chopped (ribs and seeds removed if you like) fresh red and green chiles, such as jalapeños or red Fresnos

3 tablespoons chopped fresh flat-leaf parsley

1 teaspoon crushed red pepper flakes

Kosher salt and freshly ground black pepper

Grated Parmesan cheese (optional)

A classic Italian staple. No one in America will ever pronounce it correctly, but from now on anyone can make it with ease. For a bit more spice, use some fresh red chiles.

Bring a large pot of salted water to a boil. Add the pasta, return to a boil, and cook for 8 to 10 minutes, or until tender but still firm to the bite.

Meanwhile, heat the olive oil in a heavy-bottomed skillet over medium heat. Add the garlic and chiles and cook just until the garlic turns golden brown.

Remove the skillet from the heat. Drain the pasta and transfer to the skillet with the garlic and chiles. Turn the fire on again to medium, cook for 2 minutes, and mix until the pasta is coated with the oil. Add the parsley and red pepper flakes, season with salt and pepper to taste, stir to combine, and remove from the heat.

Serve hot and, if my dad is around, grate some Parmesan on top.

Tagliatelle with
Walnut Sauce

SERVES 4

f you want to make this dish vegetarian, use veggie stock. If not, you can use either chicken or beef stock. No matter which you choose it will be delicious.

3 cups walnut pieces

2 garlic cloves, finely chopped

⅔ cup broth (see headnote)

2 tablespoons cream cheese

3 tablespoons extra-virgin olive oil

½ cup grated Parmesan cheese

1 cup heavy cream

Kosher salt and freshly ground black pepper

1 pound fresh tagliatelle

Place the walnuts, garlic, broth, cream cheese, olive oil, and Parmesan in a food processor and pulse to a smooth paste. Add the cream to make the sauce smooth, and season to taste with salt and pepper. Set aside.

Bring a large pot of salted water to a boil. Add the tagliatelle, return to a boil, and cook just until the pasta floats, about 5 minutes. Reserve about 2 tablespoons of the pasta water and drain the pasta.

Return the pasta to the pot, add the walnut sauce, and turn the heat up to medium. Toss thoroughly to coat. If the sauce gets too thick, add the reserved pasta water until it reaches the desired consistency. Remove from heat and serve immediately.

Fusilli with Sun-dried Tomatoes

2 tablespoons olive oil plus a
   bit more for drizzling
1 red onion, finely chopped
4 large garlic cloves, finely
   sliced
1½ cups sun-dried tomatoes,
   finely chopped
1 pound fusilli
3 tablespoons chopped fresh
   flat-leaf parsley
2 teaspoons chopped fresh
   thyme
1 teaspoon chopped fresh rosemary
1 cup heavy cream
12 fresh basil leaves, shredded
4 ounces grated Parmesan
   cheese

I make my own sun-dried tomatoes (page 13) and you should, too. If you live in an area where there are hot summer days, try leaving them out all day in the hot sun instead of drying them in the oven, but the oven works just fine.

Heat 2 tablespoons of the oil in a large skillet over medium heat. Add the onion and garlic and cook for about 5 minutes, or until the garlic starts to caramelize. Add the tomatoes and cook for 5 minutes more.

Meanwhile, bring a large pot of salted water to a boil. Cook the fusilli for 8 minutes, or until tender but still firm to the bite. Drain the pasta, add it to the skillet with the tomato sauce, and then add the parsley, thyme, and rosemary. Cook for a minute or two over medium heat, then add the cream. Cook until the cream reduces, 3 to 5 minutes, and the sauce has a creamy consistency. Transfer the pasta to a serving bowl or platter and garnish with basil, Parmesan, and one more drizzle of olive oil.

Artichoke and Olive Spaghetti

A classic Italian summer dish. You can use either canned or fresh artichokes; canned are fine and much less trouble.

Heat 1 tablespoon of the oil in a large skillet over low heat and gently cook the onion and garlic until golden brown. Add the tomatoes, tomato paste, and a pinch each of salt and pepper. Bring to a boil, reduce the heat, and simmer for 15 minutes, or until the tomatoes are nice and thick. Gently stir in the artichoke hearts and olives and simmer for another 5 minutes.

Add the spaghetti and cook it for two-thirds of the time indicated on the package directions. Drain well, add the remaining 2 tablespoons olive oil, and season to taste with salt and pepper. Transfer the spaghetti to the skillet with the sauce and cook for 3 minutes more over low heat. Garnish with basil and serve.

3 tablespoons extra-virgin olive oil

1 large yellow onion, chopped

3 garlic cloves, crushed

2½ cups strained canned crushed tomatoes

2 tablespoons tomato paste

Kosher salt and freshly ground black pepper

10 ounces canned artichoke hearts, drained and roughly julienned

1 cup large green olives, pitted

1 pound spaghetti

Fresh basil leaves, for garnish

Penne with Creamy Mushroom Medley

3 tablespoons butter

2 tablespoons extra-virgin olive oil

6 shallots, finely sliced

6 ounces button mushrooms, sliced

6 ounces oyster mushrooms, sliced

6 ounces chanterelle or shii-take mushrooms, sliced

Kosher salt and freshly ground black pepper

1 teaspoon garlic powder

1 teaspoon flour

3 tablespoons Marsala wine

⅔ cup heavy cream

12 ounces penne

2 tablespoons chopped fresh flat-leaf parsley

When you buy mushrooms at the store, they are already clean, so don't worry about them. But if you get them at the farmers' market PLEASE DO NOT WASH THEM IN WATER !!!! This will make them mushy and soggy. Instead, just brush them with a dry toothbrush to remove any small pieces of dirt and soil. The heat of the cooking will kill anything that might potentially harm you and the less you touch them, the better.

Melt the butter with the olive oil in a large, heavy-bottomed skillet over low heat. Add the shallots and cook over medium heat until caramelized.

Add the mushrooms and cook over low heat for 10 minutes more. Season to taste with salt and pepper and the garlic powder.

Dust the mushrooms with the flour and continue to cook on medium heat for 5 minutes, stirring, until all the water has evaporated. Add the Marsala wine and cook until it disappears.

Remove the skillet from the heat and gradually stir in the cream. Return to the heat, add additional pepper to taste and cook on low until the sauce starts to get creamy.

Meanwhile, bring a large pot of salted water to a boil. Add the penne and cook for 8 to 10 minutes. Drain the pasta and add it to the skillet with the mushroom sauce. Cook for 3 minutes over medium-low heat, then transfer to a warmed serving dish. Sprinkle with the chopped parsley and serve immediately.

Creamy Pappardelle with Broccoli

SERVES 6

You can use dry pasta for this recipe if you can't find fresh. If you do, simply cook it according to package directions ahead of time and add it to the sauce at the same time you would add the fresh pasta.

Put the butter and onion in a skillet over medium heat and cook for about 10 minutes, or until the onion has caramelized. Add the broccoli to the skillet and cook for another 5 minutes. Add the stock and the cream, bring to a boil, then simmer for 8 to 10 minutes.

Add the fresh fettuccine directly into the sauce. Lower to a simmer, and use a wooden spoon to make sure the pasta doesn't stick together too much. Season well with salt and pepper. Add the grated cheese and season with the freshly grated nutmeg. Transfer the pasta and broccoli mixture to a large, warmed serving dish and garnish with a few slices of apple. Serve immediately.

2 tablespoons butter

1 large yellow onion, finely chopped

1 pound broccoli florets

½ cup vegetable stock

½ cup heavy cream

1 pound fresh fettuccine or pappardelle

Kosher salt and ground white pepper

½ cup grated Parmesan cheese

A dash of freshly grated nutmeg

A few apple slices

Fettuccine Alfredo with Mascarpone Cream

3 tablespoons butter

⅓ cup mascarpone cheese

½ cup vegetable stock

Kosher salt and freshly ground
black pepper

1 pound fresh fettuccine

1 teaspoon freshly grated
nutmeg

1 cup freshly grated Parmesan cheese, plus extra for
serving

2 tablespoons chopped fresh
flat-leaf parsley

I never met Alfredo, but if I did I'm sure that he would be proud of
my version of this dish. It's not diet friendly, so just go with it and
then join a gym. I normally use an extra touch of black pepper
for this dish, but that's really up to you.

Melt the butter in a deep sauté pan over low heat. Mix together the
mascarpone and stock, and add to the pan. Season with salt and
pepper, and bring to a boil.

Meanwhile, bring a large pot of salted water to a boil. Add the
fettuccine and cook for 8 to 10 minutes. Reserve ½ cup of the pasta
water and drain the pasta. Return the pasta to the pot, add the sauce,
and stir to combine. Add the nutmeg and gently bring it back to a
boil, stirring with a wooden spoon. As soon as it boils, add the Parmesan, turn off the heat and keep stirring while adding the reserved
water.

Transfer the pasta mixture to a large, warmed serving plate and
garnish with the parsley. Serve immediately with the extra Parmesan cheese.

The Best Macaroni and Cheese with Parmesan Crumbs

My version of an American classic. The Parmesan crumbs add extra sharpness to the crunchy topping.

Preheat the oven to 375°F. Butter a 9 × 13-inch oven-safe dish.

Melt 2 tablespoons of the butter in a frying pan or skillet, add the bread and fry until golden brown. Set aside.

Heat the milk in a saucepan over low heat (be careful not to boil it!). While it is heating, melt the remaining 2 tablespoons butter in another pan large enough to hold all the pasta. Add the flour to the butter and cook the mixture over medium heat until it forms a smooth golden brown paste. Add the warm milk to the mixture, whisking constantly, then remove the pan from the heat and continue to stir as you add the cheddar, Fontina, and Gruyère. Place the pan back on low heat and cook until all the cheese has melted. Season with salt and pepper and garlic powder to taste.

Meanwhile, bring a large pot of salted water to a boil. Add the macaroni and cook for 4 minutes less than the package directions. Drain the pasta and stir it into the cheese sauce. Once well combined, pour the mixture into the prepared dish.

Top with the reserved fried bread pieces and the Parmesan cheese, and bake for 20 to 25 minutes. Remove from the oven, lock yourself in the kitchen, and don't let anybody in until you're done eating.

4 tablespoons (½ stick) butter, plus more for the baking dish
3 slices white sandwich bread, crusts removed, and cut into small pieces
2½ cups milk
¼ cup flour
2 cups grated white cheddar cheese
1 cup grated Fontina cheese
1½ cups grated Gruyère
Kosher salt and freshly ground black pepper
1 teaspoon garlic powder
1 pound elbow macaroni
1 cup grated Parmesan cheese

Whole Wheat Spaghetti with Ricotta

Nothing wrong with adding extra nutrients to a delicious plate of pasta by using whole wheat spaghetti, which has a different (and delicious) texture from regular pasta.

Bring a large pot of salted water to a boil. Cook the spaghetti for 8 minutes, drain, and put it back into the pot. Add the chicken stock and the mascarpone and cook for 4 to 5 minutes over high heat, until the stock has come to a boil.

Reduce the heat to medium and add the butter, ricotta, olive oil, pine nuts, salt, pepper, and Parmesan. Cook, stirring well with a wooden spoon, until the sauce has reduced to a thick and creamy consistency, 5 to 10 minutes (keep an eye on it!). Serve hot, garnished with parsley.

1 pound whole wheat spaghetti

⅓ cup chicken stock

½ cup mascarpone cheese

2 tablespoons butter

1 cup ricotta cheese

3 tablespoons olive oil

⅓ cup toasted pine nuts, crushed (try using a meat mallet or the bottom of a frying pan)

Pinch each of kosher salt and freshly ground black pepper

½ cup grated Parmesan cheese

¼ cup chopped fresh flat-leaf parsley

Spaghetti with Arugula and Almond Pesto

2 garlic cloves

1 cup whole raw almonds

1 cup arugula, packed

½ cup fresh basil leaves

½ cup grated Parmesan cheese

¼ cup extra-virgin olive oil

Kosher salt and freshly ground
black pepper

1 pound spaghetti

⅓ cup mascarpone

Pine nuts can be very expensive; almonds are just as delicious at a fraction of the cost. If you like a slightly bitter flavor, you'll love using arugula instead of 100 percent basil in this pesto.

Place the garlic, almonds, arugula, basil, Parmesan, and olive oil in the bowl of a food processor and pulse until they form a coarse paste. Season with salt and pepper to taste. Transfer to a bowl, cover, and set in the fridge.

Bring a large pot of salted water to a boil. Add the spaghetti and cook for 8 minutes, just until al dente. Drain the pasta and return it to the pot.

Off the fire, combine the pesto with the spaghetti. Then add the mascarpone, return it to the heat and cook on high for 2 minutes, stirring to coat the pasta with the sauce. Serve immediately.

Spaghetti with Crab

Thanks to America's availability of good canned crab, this dish is easy and quick and packs tons of flavor.

Bring a large pot of salted water to a boil. Add the spaghetti and cook for 4 minutes less than the package directions suggest (this will make it nice and al dente).

Leaving the pasta in the pot, drain all but about 1 cup of the pasta water. Add the olive oil, crabmeat, chives, basil, and parsley to the spaghetti and pasta water and mix until a glossy sauce forms and the pasta is well coated. Serve immediately.

1 pound spaghetti

¼ cup olive oil

½ pound jumbo lump crabmeat, thoroughly picked over and cleaned

2 tablespoons minced fresh chives

10 fresh basil leaves, chopped

2 tablespoons chopped fresh flat-leaf parsley

Spaghetti with Quick Tuna Sauce

⅓ cup extra-virgin olive oil

3 garlic cloves, finely chopped

4 ounces green or black pitted olives, sliced

12 ounces canned crushed tomatoes

1 pound Fabio's Tuna (page 55) or good quality canned tuna in olive oil

⅓ cup fish or chicken stock

2 teaspoons chopped fresh marjoram

Kosher salt and freshly ground black pepper

1 pound spaghetti

1 tablespoon chopped fresh basil

1 cup grated Parmesan cheese

This is the only way I will ever use canned tuna, but I still suggest you make some fresh, too, and try both versions to see which one you prefer.

Heat 3 tablespoons of the olive oil in a large skillet. Add the garlic and olives and cook for 5 minutes on medium-low heat. Add the tomatoes, reduce the heat to low and cook for another 15 minutes, or until some of the tomato water evaporates. Stir in the tuna, stock, marjoram, and season to taste with salt and pepper.

Cook over low heat for 5 minutes, or until heated through.

Meanwhile, bring a large pot of salted water to a boil. Add the spaghetti and cook for 8 to 10 minutes. Drain and return it to the pot, then add the sauce and basil.

Cook for another 3 to 4 minutes over low heat, stirring so that the spaghetti is coated with the sauce. As you cook, drizzle the remaining 2 tablespoons olive oil into the pasta. Serve with the grated Parmesan.

Fusilli with Smoked Salmon and Dill

2 tablespoons butter

2 tablespoons extra-virgin olive oil

1 medium red onion, finely chopped

¼ cup white wine

2 cups heavy cream

1 teaspoon chopped garlic

Kosher salt and freshly ground black pepper

12 ounces smoked salmon, finely chopped

¼ cup chopped fresh dill

Juice and pulp of 2 roasted lemon halves (see recipe page 108)

2 tablespoons sour cream

1 pound fusilli

Lemon wedges, for garnish

I f you love your morning smoked salmon with a bagel and cream cheese, you'll die for this dish—creamy, smoky, and tasty from the fresh herbs, this will be a sure winner in your home.

Heat the butter and oil in a heavy-bottomed pan over low heat. Increase the heat to medium, add the onion, and cook until softened, 4 to 5 minutes. Add the wine and continue to cook until it is about three-quarters evaporated. The time this takes depends on your stove, so you will need to watch carefully for this.

Pour in the cream, add the garlic, and season to taste with salt and pepper. Continue boiling until the sauce has reduced to a creamy consistency.

In a bowl mix the salmon, dill, lemon juice, and pulp. Add one grind of pepper and the sour cream, and mix again.

Bring a pot of salted water to a boil. Add the fusilli and cook for 10 minutes. Drain the pasta, add it to the pan with the sauce, and cook for 2 minutes more over medium heat. Stir in the salmon and cook for 1 minute more.

Serve hot with lemon wedges if you like.

Penne with Peas, Chicken, and Feta Cheese

Try adding a handful of sugar snap peas along with the frozen peas for extra sweetness.

In a large skillet, cook the shallots in the oil over medium heat for 10 to 12 minutes, until golden brown. Add the chicken, season with the salt and pepper, and continue cooking until it is completely browned and no longer pink, about 10 minutes. Add the wine and cook until it has completely evaporated.

Stir in the feta cheese along with half the scallions and season to taste with salt and pepper. If the mixture seems very dry, add a little bit of broth. Then add the peas and cook over medium heat for about 5 minutes.

Bring a pot of salted water to a boil and cook the penne for about 8 minutes, or just until al dente.

Drain the pasta, return it to the pot, and add the chicken mixture. Cook for another 2 minutes over high heat, stirring to combine the pasta and sauce well. Mix in the remaining scallions and serve.

3 tablespoons extra-virgin olive oil

6 shallots, chopped

1 pound ground chicken

½ teaspoon kosher salt

½ teaspoon freshly ground black pepper

¼ cup white wine

8 ounces feta cheese, diced

¼ cup chopped scallions

¼ cup chicken stock (if needed)

1 cup frozen peas

1 pound dried penne

Rigatoni with Spicy Chorizo, Black Olives, and Mushrooms

If chorizo is too spicy for you, try this dish with Italian sausage. It still has great flavor, but half the spiciness.

Heat the oil and butter in a large skillet over medium heat. Add the onion, garlic, olives, and shallots and cook, stirring occasionally, for 12 minutes, or until the vegetables begin to brown.

Add the mushrooms and cook, stirring occasionally, for an additional 5 minutes. Stir in the parsley and chorizo and season to taste with salt and pepper. Turn the heat down very low to keep the sauce warm while you make the pasta.

Bring a large pot of salted water to a boil. Add the rigatoni and cook for 8 minutes, just until al dente. Drain the pasta and add it to the skillet with the sauce. Increase the heat to medium, cook another 2 minutes, then serve hot topped with the queso fresco.

2 tablespoons olive oil

2 tablespoons butter

1 yellow onion, chopped

3 garlic cloves, chopped

½ cup pitted black olives

3 shallots, chopped

8 ounces oyster or shiitake mushrooms, stems removed, caps sliced

1 tablespoon chopped fresh flat-leaf parsley

12 ounces chorizo sausage, sliced or diced

Kosher salt and freshly ground black pepper

1 pound dried rigatoni

⅓ cup crumbled queso fresco

Penne with Chili Sauce, Chipotle, and Roasted Ham

2 tablespoons olive oil

3 tablespoons butter

1 red onion, chopped finely

3 garlic cloves, very finely
chopped

1 cup finely chopped ham

24 ounces canned chopped
tomatoes

2 tablespoons chopped Fresno
peppers

1 fresh red jalapeño pepper,
seeded and finely chopped

1 tablespoon chipotle chile
sauce (from chipotle chiles
in adobo)

1 pound penne

⅓ cup grated Parmesan cheese

3 tablespoons chopped fresh
flat-leaf parsley

Earthy, tasty, not so light but *so* worth it, this is a dish that will make you remember what family comfort food is all about.

Put half the oil and half the butter in a sauté pan over medium heat, add the onion and the garlic, and cook for about 12 minutes, or until they are golden brown. Add the ham and cook for 5 to 8 minutes more until the ham is starting to get lightly browned.

Add the tomatoes, chiles, jalapeños, and chipotle sauce and cook on medium-low for 30 minutes more, or until the liquid from the tomatoes has reduced and the sauce is nice and thick.

Bring a large pot of salted water to a boil and cook the penne for 8 minutes until al dente. Drain the pasta and return it to the pot. Add the sauce and cook over high heat, stirring to coat the pasta, for another 2 minutes. Toss with the Parmesan and serve with the parsley on top.

Pasta with Bacon, Tomato, and Pecorino

6 ripe medium tomatoes

3 tablespoons butter

6 slices bacon, roughly chopped

2 jalapeño peppers (green or red), seeded and chopped

1 red onion, chopped

3 garlic cloves, chopped

1 tablespoon chopped fresh thyme

Kosher salt and freshly ground black pepper

1 teaspoon chopped fresh tarragon

1 pound orecchiette

1 tablespoon extra-virgin olive oil

4 ounces grated pecorino Romano cheese

To seed the tomatoes, cut the tomatoes in half, then hold a half, face down, in one hand and squeeze it. While squeezing, rub a spoon back and forth over the open face a few times with your other hand, which will remove most of the seeds (we're not picky here).

Cut the tomatoes in half, seed them, and chop them roughly.

Melt the butter in a pan over medium heat. Add the bacon and cook until it is crispy, about 5 minutes. Add the jalapeños, onion, and garlic, and cook over medium heat for 10 minutes, or until nicely caramelized.

Add the tomatoes and thyme to the pan, then season to taste with salt and pepper and add the tarragon. Turn the heat down very low to keep the sauce warm while you make the pasta.

Bring a large pot of salted water to a boil, add the orecchiette, and cook just until al dente, 6 to 8 minutes. Drain the pasta, return it to the pot, and add the sauce. Stir to combine, then drizzle with the olive oil, and cook over medium-high heat for 2 minutes more. Mix in the pecorino and serve.

Spaghetti alla Carbonara

1 tablespoon butter, softened

⅔ pound bacon or pancetta, diced

8 egg yolks

¼ cup heavy cream

Plenty of freshly cracked black pepper

1 pound spaghetti

1 cup grated Parmesan cheese

It's no secret that I grew up not very wealthy, but nothing screams cheap and tasty like pork belly (pancetta), eggs, and some Parmesan turned into a sauce and served on a bowl of homemade spaghetti. We used to grind a Parmesan rind, but you can use store-bought spaghetti and the "good" part of the Parmesan, and you will not be disappointed.

Put the butter and the bacon or pancetta in a large, heavy skillet over medium heat and cook until crisp and browned, about 10 minutes. Transfer the meat to a plate, wipe out the pan, and place it back on the burner.

In a large bowl big enough to hold all the pasta, whisk together the egg yolks, cream, and plenty of freshly cracked black pepper.

Cook the spaghetti in a large pot of unsalted boiling water over high heat until just cooked, about 10 minutes. Reserve 1 cup of the pasta water, then drain the spaghetti. Transfer the spaghetti to the skillet over medium heat, add the pancetta, and cook for 2 to 3 minutes. Add the hot pasta to the egg yolk mixture and toss until thoroughly coated. Add the Parmesan to the pasta and toss to coat, stirring in some of the reserved cooking water to loosen the sauce and make everything creamy. Serve immediately or it will coagulate and become hard.

Entrées

YOU'VE ALREADY HAD A COCKTAIL, LITTLE APPETIZER OR SALAD, and now are ready for the main course. The main event. If you are still deciding what to make, you are thinking too hard. Keep it simple guys. Go for big, bold flavors. Stick to your ribs, unforgettable, unforgiving, non-negotiable onslaught of flavors about to tear down the walls of the Roman Coliseum. Are you pumped up now? Good!

In Italian culture, we have antipasto, a pasta course, and then our entrée, which is usually protein and starch. No salads are allowed on the meat plate. Most of the time I make the rules, but in this case, I'm just following them. An entrée is what my grandma would spend all day making—ossobuco, lamb shanks, or three whole chickens for the holidays. An entrée in my house fed everyone and their cousins. We don't mess around with entrées and neither should you.

The key to a killer entrée is all in the planning. You want to cook something that is both filling and satisfying. You don't want to make someone gain 20 pounds, but it is important to use fats and starches to your advantage, adding flavor and mouthfeel that tells your brain, "This is good, but I can't have too much of it."

For pulling the most flavor from your food, think braising, stewing, or grilling. These methods either involve a rich stock or broth to let flavors combine, or very high heat to help sear and give unbelievable texture and char to your food. Remember: full flavor! Filling and satisfying—words to live by and words to eat by.

Fried Catfish and Malt Chips

1 cup mayonnaise

2 tablespoons chopped capers

1 tablespoon chopped fresh
flat-leaf parsley

5 cups light olive oil

1½ pounds frozen French fries

1½ cups buttermilk

1½ cups flour

1½ teaspoons baking powder

1 teaspoon kosher salt

½ teaspoon freshly ground
black pepper

2 pounds catfish or cod fillet,
cut into 12 equal pieces

Kosher salt, for seasoning

1 bottle malt vinegar (you
won't use it all, so save the
rest for next time!)

2 lemons, cut into wedges, for
serving

The crisp golden fries in this recipe are the perfect complement to the catfish or cod, and if you fry them rather than bake them, no one will know you used frozen (no peeling, no slicing!). When cooling, use a rack instead of paper towels to keep them crunchy.

Combine the mayonnaise, capers, and parsley in a small bowl—homemade tartar sauce!

Place racks on two rimmed baking sheets. Set them aside. Heat the oil in a heavy-bottomed pot or deep sauté pan about 8 inches deep on medium-low until it reads just above 350°F on a deep-frying thermometer. Working in batches, fry the French fries until they are golden brown. Set them aside to cool on a rack until the fish is ready.

Pour the buttermilk into a shallow bowl. Sift the flour, baking powder, and salt and pepper together onto a platter. One by one, coat the fish pieces in buttermilk, then dredge them in the flour mixture, making sure to coat all sides. Let each one sit in the flour for a minute to help make sure they are nicely coated.

Increase the heat under the oil pot slightly so the oil temperature reaches 375°F. Carefully slip the fish into the hot oil. Depending on the size of your pot, you can fry several pieces at once, but be sure not to crowd them. Fry until golden brown, 4 to 5 minutes, turning the fish over once in a while. Transfer the fish to a rack to cool.

While they are cooling, season the French fries with salt and malt vinegar to taste. Then season the fish with salt. Serve hot with lemon wedges and your homemade tartar sauce on the side.

Salmon with Fennel and Watercress Salad

SERVES 6

Although this dish will be good with just a few hours of marinating, I really suggest you let it sit overnight for maximum flavor. For adding the Pernod, I recommend using a small plastic spray bottle, the kind you can buy in any drugstore or supermarket. Most people use them to carry their hair products with them on planes—I use them to flavor my dishes with liquors and olive oil!

PREPARE THE SALMON: Spread plastic wrap large enough to hold the salmon with plenty of extra room around it on a counter or tabletop. Combine the sugar, salt, and mustard powder in a bowl. Sprinkle two handfuls of this mixture onto the plastic wrap, then place the bottom of the salmon fillet on it.

Sprinkle the remaining sugar-salt mixture, the fennel seeds, and the dill onto the salmon. Spray or drizzle with the Pernod, then cover the entire salmon tightly with the plastic wrap and put it on a rimmed platter or baking sheet. Refrigerate for at least 12 hours.

PAN-ROAST THE LEMONS: Preheat the oven to 425°F. Line a half sheet pan or rimmed baking sheet with parchment paper.

Heat the olive oil in a small skillet over medium-high heat. Add the lemon halves, cut side down, and cook until the lemons are golden brown, 5 to 7 minutes. Set the lemon halves aside.

Remove the plastic wrap and use a wet paper towel to scrape the seasoning mixture off the salmon. Run the salmon under cold running water for a few seconds, pat dry with paper towels, and cut the fish into 6 equal portions. Lightly coat the fish with olive oil and place on the prepared pan. Roast the fish in the oven for 12 minutes.

WHILE THE SALMON COOKS, MAKE THE DRESSING: In a small bowl whisk together the olive oil, mustard seeds, honey, and lemon juice.

Salmon

1⅓ cups sugar

1 cup kosher salt

2 teaspoons dry mustard powder

1 whole side of salmon, skinless (2 to 3 pounds)

⅓ cup fennel seeds

½ cup fresh dill, minced

⅔ cup Pernod

¼ cup extra-virgin olive oil

Pan-roasted Lemons

1 tablespoon olive oil

2 lemons, halved

Dressing

3 tablespoons extra-virgin olive oil

2 teaspoons brown mustard seeds

1 tablespoon honey

1 tablespoon fresh lemon juice

Salad

1 pound watercress, washed and dried, large stems removed

1 fennel bulb, trimmed and
   sliced as thinly as possible,
   or shaved with a mandoline
1 cup shaved Parmesan cheese

In a large bowl, combine the watercress, fennel, and Parmesan with all the dressing and toss.

Remove the salmon from the oven, place each portion on a plate and serve with the dressed salad on the side.

Baked Halibut with Spinach, Orange, and Pistachio

SERVES 4

Many of you have probably realized by now that I am not big into anything French. But I did learn from a dear French friend how to supreme oranges, which is very easy and rewarding (especially if you, like me, *hate* to peel citrus and then still have to deal with that white fuzzy covering). With a *really sharp* knife, remove the skin of each orange from the top to the bottom in sections, just like you would peel a banana. Then slice the segments out of the orange by cutting in between each section membrane. The juicy part will come out and the membranes will stay intact.

3 tablespoons olive oil

Four 6-ounce pieces skinless halibut (you can use cod, too)

Kosher salt and freshly ground black pepper

1 tablespoon white wine vinegar

1 tablespoon honey

3 oranges

½ cup chopped pistachios

2 cups baby spinach, roughly chopped

Heat 1 tablespoon of the oil in a large skillet over medium-high heat. Season the fish with salt and pepper, and cook in the oil until light brown, 2 to 4 minutes per side.

In a large bowl, whisk together the vinegar, honey, remaining 2 tablespoons oil, and season with salt and pepper.

Cut away the peel and white pith of the orange and slice the orange into rounds. Place them in a baking dish along with the pistachios and spinach, and gently toss to combine. Place the fish on top.

Bake at 425°F for 5 minutes.

Sautéed Sea Bass with Romesco Sauce

2 medium red bell peppers

1 dried ancho pepper, stemmed and seeded

½ teaspoon kosher salt

1½ tablespoons slivered almonds, toasted

1 tablespoon extra-virgin olive oil

1 tablespoon red wine vinegar

¼ teaspoon sugar

¼ teaspoon freshly ground black pepper

⅛ teaspoon crushed red pepper flakes

2 garlic cloves, chopped

1 slice whole wheat bread

Four 6-ounce sea bass fillets, skin removed

Light olive oil

4 lemon wedges, for serving

Romesco is another one of those sauces that can be made ahead and in large batches for later use. If you like some spice, I suggest you add 1 tablespoon of chipotle pepper in adobo sauce (about one-quarter of a can) for extra kick.

Preheat the oven to 425°F.

Cut the bell peppers in half from top to bottom; remove and discard the seeds and membranes.

Place the peppers, skin side up, on a rimmed baking sheet and flatten by pressing each one down with the palm of your hand until it cracks. Roast for about 10 minutes, or until blackened. Add the ancho pepper to the sheet, turn the oven to broil, and broil all of the peppers for 2 minutes.

Place the bell peppers in a metal or glass bowl tightly covered with plastic wrap. Let stand 5 minutes, then remove each pepper and peel it by pulling the skin off with your fingers (it will release easily after the cooking and steaming). Place the bell peppers, ancho pepper, and ¼ teaspoon of the salt into a food processor along with the almonds, olive oil, vinegar, sugar, black pepper, red pepper flakes, garlic, and bread, in that order. Process until smooth.

Heat a large skillet over medium-high heat. Sprinkle the remaining ¼ teaspoon salt over the fish. Coat the skillet with light oil. Add the fish to the skillet and cook for 6 minutes per side on medium-high heat. Top with the sauce and serve with lemon wedges.

"Two-Minute" Squid and Cherry Tomatoes

SERVES 4 TO 6

Be sure to use a cast-iron or other metal pan for this recipe. It won't work with nonstick. Also, it goes great with crusty bread, so buy a loaf when you're out shopping for ingredients. And yes, you're actually cooking the squid for 5 minutes—nothing in the kitchen actually takes 2 minutes!—but the point is it's fast and dinner is done!

Heat a large sauté pan or cast-iron skillet over high heat until very, very hot. Combine the squid, olive oil, garlic, parsley, marjoram, red pepper flakes, basil, salt, and pepper in a bowl and mix together. Add to the pan, shake once, then let sit for 2 minutes until the calamari starts to get nice and brown. Turn the pieces and cook for 3 minutes more.

Add the tomatoes and lemon juice to the pan, stir to combine, cook for 1 minute more. Serve with crusty bread.

1 pound cleaned squid, patted dry and sliced into rounds (use the legs, too)

⅓ cup olive oil

4 garlic cloves, finely chopped

2 tablespoons chopped fresh flat-leaf parsley

2 tablespoons chopped fresh marjoram

2 teaspoons crushed red pepper flakes

½ cup packed basil leaves

Kosher salt and freshly ground black pepper

20 to 30 cherry tomatoes, halved and seeds squeezed out

2 tablespoons fresh lemon juice

Old Bay Clams and Crab Bake from Maryland

SERVES 8 TO 10

I can easily eat an entire recipe of these all by myself. And please, *please* drink a light beer with it, like Blue Moon or Corona—it's not very Maryland but *sooooo* refreshing. Keep a wet towel handy, too—it will get messy!

Place a steamer basket in a 30-quart pot. Add the wine and water, cover, and bring to a boil. Add the potatoes, cover again, and cook 5 minutes.

Add the lobsters, cover, and cook 10 minutes. Gently place the corn, celery, sausage, lemons, and garlic into the pot. Cover and cook 10 minutes. Add the thyme and the clams, cover, and cook 10 minutes. Add the mussels, cover, and cook until they open, about 5 minutes more. Discard any shellfish that do not open.

Using a slotted spoon and tongs, remove the contents of the pot from the broth and place on a very large platter. As soon as the fish hits the platter sprinkle with Old Bay.

Ladle the broth from the pot into small bowls, making sure to avoid the sandy sediment at the bottom of the pot, and divide the crabmeat evenly among the bowls.

Serve the clambake with the bowls of broth and melted butter for dipping.

½ bottle dry white wine

10 cups water

2 pounds really small red potatoes

4 live lobsters, about 1¼ pounds each

4 ears of corn, halved

3 celery stalks, cut into 1½-inch pieces

2 pounds of chorizo or linguiça sausage, cut into 1-inch rounds

2 lemons, cut into wedges

20 garlic cloves

1 large bunch thyme

4 pounds littleneck, Manila, or steamer clams, scrubbed

2 pounds mussels, scrubbed and debearded

¼ cup Old Bay seasoning

1 pound cleaned lump crabmeat

½ pound (2 sticks) butter, melted

Shrimp Roast

Spice Blend

1 teaspoon ground coriander

1 teaspoon ground cumin

½ teaspoon garam masala

½ teaspoon fennel seeds,
   crushed

2 teaspoons peeled, minced
   fresh ginger

Shrimp

5 small dried jalapeño or ser-
   rano chiles, stems removed

1 cup hot water

2 pounds medium shrimp,
   peeled and cleaned

1 teaspoon hot chili powder

¼ teaspoon coarsely ground
   black pepper

1 teaspoon kosher salt

¼ cup olive oil

1 medium onion, diced

4 garlic cloves, minced

1 tablespoon tomato paste

½ cup scallions, green parts,
   trimmed to 1 inch and
   chopped

You can also make this dish on the BBQ in summer by combining the shrimp and all the other ingredients in a large bowl, then putting them in a pouch of aluminum foil, placing it on the grill and closing the top.

MAKE THE SPICE BLEND: In a small bowl mix the coriander, cumin, garam masala, fennel seeds, and ginger until well combined.

MAKE THE SHRIMP: Put the dried chiles in a small saucepan with the hot water. Let them soak for 5 minutes, then drain and mince them. Set aside.

Pat the shrimp dry with paper towels and put them into a medium bowl.

Add the chili powder, black pepper, and salt and toss to coat.

Heat the olive oil in a skillet or wok over medium heat. Add the onions and sauté until they begin to brown. Add the garlic, tomato paste, and reserved minced soaked, dried chiles and cook for 1 minute.

Add the spice blend and fry briefly until it begins to crackle. Increase the heat to high and add the shrimp, stirring constantly until the shrimp are cooked through, about 5 minutes. Transfer to a serving dish. Top with the scallions just before serving.

Shrimp and Grits with Chorizo from Old Friends in South Carolina

Shrimp

3 slices bacon

1½ pounds unpeeled, medium raw shrimp

1 teaspoon kosher salt

½ teaspoon freshly ground black pepper

¼ cup flour

½ cup chopped scallions

2 tablespoons olive oil

1 cup sliced fresh cremini mushrooms

4 garlic cloves, minced

2 tablespoons fresh lime juice

½ tablespoon sauce from a can of chipotle peppers in adobo sauce

Cheese Grits

1½ cups chicken stock

1 cup heavy cream

1 cup fully cooked chorizo, crumbled

1 teaspoon kosher salt

1 cup uncooked quick-cooking grits or polenta

6 ounces cheddar cheese, shredded

1 tablespoon butter

½ cup grated Parmesan cheese

Kosher salt and freshly ground black pepper

The light stir-frying of the shrimp ingredients makes all the difference once they are poured over some hot steamy grits.

MAKE THE SHRIMP: Cook bacon in a large nonstick skillet over medium heat until crisp. Remove from the skillet, crumble, and set aside. Leave the fat in the pan.

Peel the shrimp and devein, if desired. Sprinkle the shrimp with salt and pepper. Place the flour in a shallow bowl or plate and dredge the shrimp in it. Heat the skillet with the bacon fat over medium heat, add the shrimp and sauté in the fat until they turn pink; just a few minutes. Add the scallions and sauté another 2 minutes, remove from skillet, and set aside.

In the same skillet you used for the shrimp, heat the olive oil, add the mushrooms and garlic, and sauté until they are caramelized. Return the cooked shrimp and the bacon to the skillet. Stir in the lime juice and chipotle sauce and cook 3 minutes more, stirring to loosen particles from bottom of skillet. Set aside.

MAKE THE CHEESE GRITS: Combine the stock, heavy cream, chorizo, and salt in a medium saucepan and bring to a boil over medium-high heat. Gradually whisk in the grits. Reduce the heat to low and simmer, stirring occasionally, for about 10 minutes, or until the grits have thickened. Stir in cheddar cheese, butter, and Parmesan, and season to taste with salt and pepper. Serve hot.

Buttermilk Fried Chicken

SERVES 3 TO 4

This chicken marinates overnight in buttermilk and other delicious flavors so be sure to start a day ahead.

Mix together the buttermilk, rosemary sprigs, and garlic in a bowl or container large enough to hold all the chicken pieces. Add the chicken; cover and let it marinate overnight in the fridge.

Mix 3 cups of the flour, the paprika, black pepper, and mustard powder together in a rectangular dish that is large enough to hold all the chicken.

Drain the chicken from the buttermilk, and roll the wet chicken in the flour mixture. After dredging, let the chicken rest for at least 15 minutes.

In a deep sauté pan, heat enough light oil to cover the chicken pieces to 350°F. While it heats, place a rack over a rimmed baking sheet.

Dust the lemon slices in the remaining ¼ cup flour and set aside.

When the oil reaches temperature, fry the chicken for 8 to 10 minutes, turning the chicken to get even color, then add the rosemary, sage, and floured lemon slices to the oil. Continue to fry for 7 to 10 minutes more.

Remove the chicken from the oil, transfer to the rack to drain. If the herbs are very dark and burned you can discard them. Otherwise they are good to munch on. Season the chicken with salt and black pepper and serve.

3 cups buttermilk

3 to 5 rosemary sprigs

8 garlic cloves, crushed

1 whole chicken, cut into 16 pieces

3 cups plus ¼ cup flour

2 tablespoons smoked paprika

2 tablespoons freshly ground black pepper

1 tablespoon dry mustard powder

Light olive oil, for frying

1 lemon, sliced into thin rounds

3 fresh rosemary sprigs

3 fresh sage sprigs

Kosher salt and freshly ground black pepper

Chicken Potpies

Crust

1¾ cups flour

½ cup grated Parmesan cheese

1 teaspoon sugar

1 teaspoon kosher salt

12 tablespoons (1½ sticks)
  cold butter, cut into small
  chunks

¼ cup ice water

Filling

½ cup extra-virgin olive oil

1 cup diced celery

1 cup diced onions

1 cup diced carrot

1 teaspoon kosher salt plus
  more if needed

¼ teaspoon freshly ground
  black pepper

1 cup diced potatoes (no need
  to peel)

4 boneless, skinless chicken
  breasts, cut into bite-size
  cubes

¾ cup flour

2¼ cups chicken stock

1 cup diced broccoli

½ cup peas, fresh if possible
  but frozen is fine

Most people try to make these little individual ramekins of joy prettier by pressing a fork all around the side to "mark" the dough. I say forget it—leave the dough hanging from the side and eat it! Why waste it? You'll need it anyway since every time I have a potpie, I always wish to have an extra bite of the pastry on the side.

MAKE THE CRUST: Place the flour, Parmesan, sugar, and salt in the bowl of a food processor and pulse a few times to combine. Add the butter and pulse until the mixture looks like fine gravel. With the motor running, slowly add the ice water through the feed tube, and process just until the dough comes together.

Transfer the dough quickly to a lightly floured surface, and knead it briefly a few times until it forms a ball. Flatten the ball slightly, then wrap the dough in plastic wrap and refrigerate it while you make the filling.

MAKE THE FILLING: In a pot, heat the olive oil over medium-high heat. Add the celery, onions, and carrots and season with a pinch of salt and pepper. Sauté, stirring occasionally, just until the mixture starts to caramelize.

Add the potatoes and sauté until the potatoes start to brown around the edges and the onions are a little more caramelized.

Stir in the chicken along with another pinch of salt and pepper, and continue to sauté, stirring occasionally, until all the meat turns white, about 10 minutes.

Sprinkle the flour over the chicken and vegetables, stirring well so that the flour evenly coats the mixture, and cook for 1 minute, stirring constantly.

— {Continued} —

2 fresh flat-leaf parsley sprigs,
    chopped
2 fresh oregano sprigs,
    chopped
2 eggs

Gradually stir in the chicken broth and bring to a boil over medium heat, stirring constantly, then simmer for 1 minute.

Stir in the broccoli and then the peas and cook to heat through. Remove the pot from the heat and stir in the parsley and oregano. Season with more salt and pepper to taste.

ASSEMBLE THE POTPIES: Preheat the oven to 400°F.

In a small bowl, whisk together the eggs with a pinch of salt and a little water, and set aside.

On a lightly floured surface, roll the dough to a ⅓-inch thickness. Cut out 6 rounds that are slightly larger than 6 oven-safe bowls.

Ladle the hot filling into the bowls. Top each bowl with a round of dough, making sure it touches the filling and letting the extra hang over the side. Brush each dough top with the prepared egg wash then cut small slits in them to let steam escape.

Place the bowls on a baking sheet, and bake until the pastry is golden brown and the filling is bubbly, 30 to 45 minutes. Let stand for 5 minutes before serving.

Quick Chicken Parmigiana

SERVES 4

This has got to be America's most beloved Italian-inspired dish (though you should *never* serve this with pasta on the side. Don't ask why—it's just the way we do it in Italy. No chicken with pasta!). If you want to make it a bit cheaper and even more delicious, buy a piece of Parmesan with the rind on it and, instead of cutting it away, grate the rind. We used to do this in Italy to save money, and the rind is 100 percent edible. Even better, it tastes like Parmesan on steroids because it has very little moisture inside and works great for oven cooking because it won't make the chicken soggy like most cheeses.

2 cups panko or fine plain bread crumbs

½ cup grated pecorino Romano cheese

Kosher salt and freshly ground black pepper

1 cup flour

4 eggs, lightly beaten

1 pound chicken cutlets or small chicken breasts, pounded to ⅛-inch thickness

½ cup light olive oil

2 cups marinara sauce, plus more for serving

1½ cups grated mozzarella cheese

1 cup grated Parmesan cheese

Chopped fresh basil, for garnish

Combine the bread crumbs and pecorino Romano in a small bowl and season with salt and pepper.

Put the flour, the eggs, and the bread-crumb mixture into three separate shallow dishes. Dip each piece of chicken in flour, shake off the excess, then dip in egg and let excess drip off before dredging in bread crumbs to coat.

Preheat the oven to 400°F.

Heat the olive oil in deep sauté pan or skillet over medium-high heat. Cook the cutlets for 3 to 4 minutes per side, until they are golden brown. As each breast is cooked place on a platter and set aside.

In a baking dish large enough to hold the chicken breasts in a single layer, lay down the cutlets and top them with the marinara sauce, then the mozzarella, and finally the Parmesan. Bake for 10 minutes, or until the mozzarella starts to melt. Sprinkle the chopped basil (optional) over the dish and serve.

Apple-Walnut Salad Over Fried Chicken Cutlet

SERVES 4

A little bit of sin, a little bit of salad. The crunch of the apples and the freshness of the greens and citrus are the perfect way to cut the richness of these cutlets.

Dust the chicken with the flour and tap it off.

Season the chicken with salt and pepper. Heat 1 tablespoon of the olive oil in a large sauté pan over medium heat, add the chicken, and cook until it is tender and browned all over, about 4 minutes per side.

Mix together the olive oil, sour cream, mustard, and lemon juice until smooth and well combined, then season with salt and pepper. Add the celery, apple, walnuts, and toss to combine; fold in the chives.

Serve the salad with the chicken.

8 chicken cutlets

¼ cup flour

Kosher salt and freshly ground black pepper

3 tablespoons extra-virgin olive oil

¼ cup low-fat sour cream

1 teaspoon stone-ground mustard

1 tablespoon fresh lemon juice

2 celery stalks, thinly sliced on the diagonal

2 apples, cored, seeded, and sliced into thin half-moons (red or red Delicious apples work well)

½ cup chopped walnuts

1 tablespoon chopped fresh chives

Curried Chicken Thighs with Pineapple Mint Skewers

1 cup unsweetened coconut milk

½ cup creamy almond butter

2 tablespoons molasses

2 tablespoons red curry paste

2 tablespoons fresh lime juice

1 tablespoon yellow curry powder

½ tablespoon kosher salt

1 pound boneless, skinless chicken thighs, cut in 1½-inch × 1½-inch cubes

1 fresh pineapple, peeled and diced

3 tablespoons extra-virgin olive oil

3 tablespoons chopped fresh mint

This is a great dish for parties, easy to eat and carry around—just don't jump in the pool with it! You can replace the pineapple with peaches or mango if you prefer. Don't forget the chicken needs to marinate overnight.

In a bowl, combine the coconut milk, almond butter, molasses, red curry paste, lime juice, yellow curry powder, and salt. Place half of the sauce in a zip-top bag with the chicken and marinate overnight in the refrigerator. Keep the rest of the sauce in a covered container overnight in the fridge for basting while you cook.

Preheat the oven to 375°F. On metal skewers, alternate pieces of chicken with chunks of pineapple. Place skewers on a rack over a baking sheet and bake for about 20 minutes, basting every 5 minutes with the remaining sauce.

When the chicken is done, transfer it to a platter. Mix the pan juices with the olive oil and mint and pour the sauce over the skewers just before serving.

Roasted Pork Shoulder with Tuscan Salmoriglio Sauce

In Italian *salmoriglio* means "briny" or lightly salted. In the old days, this sauce was used to cover the smell of meats that hadn't been stored properly. Today it is simply a tasty accompaniment that will make your mouth water. For beginner cooks, I recommend using boneless cuts, but I prefer cooking with bone-in meats.

MAKE THE PORK: Rub the pork with salt and sugar, wrap it in plastic wrap, and let it rest overnight in the refrigerator.

Preheat the oven to 300°F.

With a wet cloth, wipe the remaining sugar and salt from the pork. Put the oregano, thyme, anchovies, and a pinch of salt and pepper in a food processor and blend into a fine paste. Rub the paste all over the meat.

Pour the olive oil in a pot or casserole large enough to hold the pork and turn the heat to medium. Add the meat and brown it on all sides. Add the stock, cover the pot, and transfer it to the oven. Roast the pork until it is fork-tender, about 3½ hours.

MAKE THE SALMORIGLIO: Combine the garlic, pine nuts, shallots, mint, thyme, parsley, lemon juice, olive oil, salt, pepper, and onion powder either in a food processor or in a bowl with a whisk.

To serve, slice the meat in thick slices (a serrated knife works well) and drizzle with the salmoriglio.

Pork

One 4-pound boneless pork shoulder
½ cup kosher salt
⅔ cup sugar
3 tablespoons fresh oregano
3 tablespoons fresh thyme
10 anchovy fillets, chopped
Freshly ground black pepper
3 tablespoons olive oil
⅓ cup beef or vegetable stock

Salmoriglio Sauce

3 garlic cloves, minced
¼ cup pine nuts
2 shallots, finely minced
10 fresh mint leaves, minced
2 tablespoons minced fresh thyme
2 tablespoons minced fresh flat-leaf parsley
Juice of 2 lemons
1 cup extra-virgin olive oil
Kosher salt and freshly ground black pepper
1 tablespoon onion powder

Ham-and-Cheese-Stuffed Pork Chops

SERVES 4

You should use bone-in pork chops that are not center cut for this recipe. The fattier the pork chop, the better.

Preheat the oven to 375°F.

Slice a 2-inch pocket into the side of each pork chop, making sure you go deep enough into the chop to create enough space for the stuffing. Stuff each one with 2 slices of ham and 2 of cheese. Don't be afraid to overstuff them!

Place the chopped rosemary and sage, a drizzle of olive oil, and some salt and pepper in a large plastic bag and add the pork chops. Marinate them this way at room temperature for at least an hour.

When you're ready to cook the chops, place a large skillet over high heat. Add a drizzle of olive oil to the skillet and sear the pork chops on one side until they are well caramelized, 3 to 5 minutes. Flip them, season the cooked sides with the salt and pepper, then caramelize the other sides for another 3 to 5 minutes.

Place the pork chops in the oven and finish cooking. When their internal temperature registers 160°F, they'll be just medium and ready to eat.

Four 12-ounce pork chops
8 slices ham
8 slices mozzarella or Fontina cheese
2 tablespoons chopped fresh rosemary
2 tablespoons chopped fresh sage
¼ cup extra-virgin olive oil
½ teaspoon kosher salt plus more for seasoning
½ teaspoon freshly ground black pepper plus more for seasoning

Ham Pie

1 pound ground pork

1 teaspoon garlic powder

1 teaspoon onion powder

1 teaspoon chili powder

6 ounces Italian sausage meat

1 pound ham, cut in small
 cubes

1½ teaspoons chopped fresh
 sage

1½ teaspoons chopped fresh
 rosemary

1 red onion, finely chopped

Kosher salt and freshly ground
 black pepper

3 cups flour (and a little extra
 for dusting)

2 teaspoons kosher salt

⅔ cup water

¼ cup milk

8 tablespoons (1 stick) butter
 plus more for the pan

3 egg yolks, lightly beaten

I don't have much to say about this dish because I'm usually too busy eating it to think about it. It's a meat paradise for people who've worked hard all day and deserve a meal that would satisfy a T. rex.

Preheat the oven to 350°F. Grease the bottom of an 8- or 9-inch springform pan and dust with flour. Line the springform pan with parchment paper.

Combine the ground pork with the garlic powder, onion powder, and chili powder in a large bowl, then add the sausage, ham, sage, rosemary, and onion. Season with salt and pepper and mix well.

In a medium bowl combine the flour with the salt. In a saucepan over low heat add the milk and butter with the water and heat until the butter melts. Lower the heat as much as possible, then add the flour mixture and stir until it forms a firm ball. Let the dough cool to room temperature, then remove it from the pan and work into smooth dough on the countertop. If the dough is too sticky dust it with up to 1 tablespoon of additional flour.

Set aside one-third of the dough. On a floured surface, roll out the remaining dough into a 12-inch circle. Line the pan with the dough, leaving some to hang over the edge. Fill the pan with the meat mixture and press down, eliminating any air bubbles. Roll out the rest of the dough into an 8- or 9-inch circle (depending on the size of the pan) that fits on the pie and cover the pie with it. Tuck in the edges of the dough.

Cut 5 to 6 slits in the top crust. Brush the crust with the beaten egg yolks and bake the pie for 30 minutes. Reduce the oven temperature to 320°F, and bake the pie for another hour. Transfer the pie to a rack to cool. When it is completely cool run a knife between the pie and the sides of the pan and remove the sides.

Pork Roast Braised with Sweet Wine and Oranges

SERVES 8

A sauvignon blanc or chardonnay work well for this dish. You want to use wine that is not too dry.

Preheat the oven to 400°F.

Combine the garlic, rosemary, and tarragon with a pinch each of salt and pepper. Rub it all over the meat.

Pour the olive oil into a baking dish, then put in the meat. Place in the oven and cook for 10 to 15 minutes.

While the meat is cooking, heat the vegetable stock to boiling. Remove the pan from the oven, add the stock and the oranges. Reduce the oven temperature to 300°F and return the pork to the oven. Continue cooking, uncovered, for 2½ to 3 hours, basting with the wine every 30 minutes.

When the meat is done, transfer it from the pan to a carving board. Add the bread crumbs to the pan juices and stir to combine. Slice the meat and serve it on a platter with the bread-crumb sauce over it.

3 garlic cloves, crushed

2 tablespoons fresh rosemary

2 tablespoons minced fresh tarragon

Kosher salt and freshly ground black pepper

5 pounds boneless pork roast

3 tablespoons extra-virgin olive oil

½ cup vegetable stock

5 oranges divided into segments, or 2 cups drained canned mandarin oranges

½ cup sweet white wine

1 cup panko bread crumbs

Arizona Pulled Pork Chimichanga

SERVES 6

Y ou'll be amazed by how delicious and moist the pork is for these chimichangas. Save the braising liquid and pour it over the fried shell for serving.

Combine the coriander, cumin, and chili powder in a large bowl. Add the pork and combine well with your hands to make sure the pieces are well coated with the spices.

Put ¼ cup of the light olive oil and the pork into a Dutch oven or casserole over medium heat. Add the garlic and cook until the meat has browned on all sides, about 15 minutes. Pour in half of the beer and reduce the heat to low. Add the vinegar and, using a spoon, scrape up any brown bits from the bottom of the pan. Cover and cook for about 1 hour, or until the pork is fork-tender and most of the pan juices have evaporated.

Once the pork is cooked, turn off the heat and use a fork to shred the pork. Leave it in the pan in whatever juices are left.

In a blender, combine the tomatillos, onion, parsley, chipotles, and remaining beer and purée until smooth. Season with salt and black pepper.

Combine the sauce and the remaining ¼ cup light olive oil in a pot over low heat and simmer for 20 to 25 minutes until piping hot. Combine it with the pork mixture.

Heat the oil for frying in a deep sauté pan to 375°F.

Place some cheddar in the middle of each tortilla (about 1 ounce is right), spread it evenly over the whole surface, then place some pork (about 2½ ounces) on it. Fold the top and bottom parts of the tortilla up just barely over the pork, then roll it up sideways, burrito-style.

Fry until golden, about 5 minutes, and serve.

1 teaspoon whole coriander seeds

1 teaspoon ground cumin

1 teaspoon chili powder

2½ pounds boneless pork shoulder, roughly cut into 2-inch chunks

½ cup light olive oil

6 garlic cloves, smashed

2 cups of blonde beer (I like Corona)

1 tablespoon balsamic vinegar

4 tomatillos, seeded and cut into quarters

2 red onions, roughly chopped

1 cup fresh flat-leaf parsley leaves

One 7-ounce can chipotle peppers in adobo sauce

Kosher salt and freshly ground black pepper

3 cups light olive oil, for frying

1½ cups shredded cheddar cheese

Six 12-inch flour tortillas

Balsamic Kansas-Style Ribs

SERVES 6

Marinating the ribs overnight is best if you can manage it. For this recipe you need to have a smoke box or a grill that allows you to smoke meats. The way I like to do this is to preheat the grill to 325°F and place several wood chips in it (you can soak your chips in beer if you like). The slowly burning chips will add flavor to the meat as it is cooking.

MAKE THE RUB: Place the salt, onion powder, chili powder, celery salt, garlic powder, cumin seeds, freshly ground black pepper, ground turmeric, and mustard seeds in a spice grinder or mortar and mix and crush them until they are well combined.

Combine the spice mixture with the brown sugar, cinnamon, and nutmeg and mix well. Set aside.

PREPARE THE RIBS: Cut each rib rack in half, then pour the vinegar over them and rub it in well, making sure you cover all the meat. Place the ribs in a pan and let them rest in the vinegar for about an hour, turning them back and forth every 15 minutes. They do not need to be refrigerated for this step. Remove them from the vinegar and let them dry for about 30 minutes more.

Press the rub mixture into the ribs, coating them well. Seal the ribs in large zip-top bags and refrigerate for at least 3 hours, or up to overnight.

Grill the meat at 325°F for about 2 hours, or until the meat can be pulled off the bone easily with your fingers.

Rub

1 tablespoon kosher salt
1 tablespoon onion powder
1 tablespoon chili powder
1 tablespoon celery salt
1 tablespoon garlic powder
1 tablespoon cumin seeds
1 tablespoon freshly ground black pepper
1 tablespoon ground turmeric
1 tablespoon mustard seeds
3 tablespoons brown sugar
⅓ teaspoon ground cinnamon
½ teaspoon freshly ground nutmeg, (but pre-ground is fine, too)

Ribs

4 pounds baby back pork ribs
2 cups balsamic vinegar

Pork Loin Cooked in Milk with Pistachio

5 tablespoons (½ stick plus 1
tablespoon) butter

2 red onions, finely chopped

¼ pound thinly sliced roasted
ham, finely chopped

6 garlic cloves, crushed

2 teaspoons fennel seeds

3 teaspoons chopped fresh
marjoram

½ cup pistachio nuts

One 2-pound boneless pork
loin, tied

Kosher salt and freshly ground
black pepper

4 cups milk

1 cup heavy cream

If you like your sauce a little thicker, you can add a bit of corn-starch to this one for extra creaminess. Stir it in at the end, a tablespoon at a time, and whisk for 5 to 10 minutes until the sauce has reached the consistency you like.

Melt the butter over medium heat in a Dutch oven large enough to hold the pork loin. Add the onions and the ham and cook until the onions are caramelized. Add the garlic, fennel seeds, and marjoram and cook for 5 minutes more, then add the pistachio nuts.

Rub the meat with salt and pepper, and add it to the pot to brown. In the meantime, heat the milk to the boiling point in a small saucepan.

When the meat has browned, pour the milk over it. Let it simmer on low for an hour or a little longer, until the milk has reduced by about half.

Add the heavy cream and turn the meat over, then let it cook and reduce for another 30 to 45 minutes until the meat is fully cooked and tender.

Remove the meat from the pan, cut off the twine, and slice into medallions. Serve the medallions with the pan sauce spooned over them.

Shish Kebabs with Basil-Yogurt and Parmesan Sauce

SERVES 6

These are the perfect party food and great served with some grilled pita chips or grilled tortillas.

PREPARE THE LAMB: Combine the thyme, rosemary, garlic, onion, spicy pepper, and oil in a bowl and mix well to create a marinade. Season the lamb with salt and black pepper, place in a pan or bowl, and cover with the marinade. Refrigerate overnight.

MAKE THE FLATBREAD: In a bowl, mix together the flour, water, and salt. Set aside for 30 minutes to let it rise. Divide the risen dough into 6 equal pieces, shape each one into a ball, then flatten and roll into disks. Cook each side over a very high heat in a frying pan *without oil* for 1 to 2 minutes until the dough starts to bubble, blisters a little, and turns golden brown.

MAKE THE SAUCE: Combine the yogurt, basil, cumin, garlic, salt, and Parmesan in a bowl. Set aside.

Place the meat on skewers. Barbecue or grill at 350°F, turning the skewers about every 3 to 4 minutes, until they are evenly cooked and a bit charred on the outside.

To serve, wrap a flatbread around each skewer to use to pull the meat off, place the flatbread and lamb on a plate and then drizzle with the sauce.

Lamb

2 tablespoons finely chopped fresh thyme

½ cup roughly chopped fresh rosemary

6 garlic cloves, crushed and finely chopped

1 red onion, finely chopped

1 spicy pepper such as habanero or Scotch bonnet, seeds and stems removed and finely chopped

¼ cup olive oil

Kosher salt and freshly ground black pepper

One 2-pound boneless leg of lamb, cut into cubes

Flatbread

11 ounces whole wheat or all-purpose flour

¾ cup water

1 teaspoon kosher salt

Sauce

2½ cups plain yogurt

1 cup finely chopped fresh basil

1 teaspoon ground cumin

½ garlic clove, mashed in a mortar with a pestle, or very finely chopped

Pinch of kosher salt

½ cup grated Parmesan cheese

Skirt Steak with Crispy Oven Fries

Spice Mix
2 teaspoons onion powder

2 teaspoons garlic powder

2 teaspoons ground white
   pepper

2 teaspoons dried rosemary

1 teaspoon finely chopped
   fresh sage

French Fries
¼ cup extra-light olive oil

1 pound frozen French fries

Kosher salt and freshly ground
   black pepper

2 tablespoons spice mix

Steak
2 pounds skirt steak, cut in
   half crosswise

Remaining spice mix

I always have frozen French fries on hand, which I like to make in the oven tossed with light olive oil and the same spice blend I use for this skirt steak. They're a tasty time-saver when I'm in a hurry. They have a great flavor and a crunch that's close to homemade fries, with fewer calories. Along with sautéed spinach (see recipe, page 164), they're the perfect side. The trick to skirt steak—a really flavorful but more often than not a bit chewy cut —is to slice it across the grain and reseason with the spice mix before serving.

Preheat the oven to 350°F.

MAKE THE SPICE MIX: In a small bowl combine the onion powder, garlic powder, white pepper, rosemary, and sage.

MAKE THE FRENCH FRIES: In a large bowl combine the oil and the fries. Season with salt and black pepper and 2 tablespoons of the spice mix. Toss and turn the fries until they are coated in the spices and oil, then put them on a roasting pan and bake for about 15 to 20 minutes until they are golden brown.

MAKE THE STEAK: Season the steaks on both sides with 2 teaspoons of the spice mix; reserve the remaining mix.

Heat a cast-iron skillet or stainless steel frying pan over medium-high heat until very hot. No oil needed! Add the steak and cook for about 3 minutes on each side, until caramelized; the meat will be cooked to medium. Remove the meat from the pan and let it rest for 5 minutes on a cutting board before slicing.

Thinly slice the steaks across the grain, sprinkle with the remaining spice mix, and serve with sautéed spinach and hot French fries.

Roast Prime Rib of Beef with Best Little Yorkshire Puddings

I favor roasting large cuts of meat at a low temperature so that the gentle heat cooks them evenly throughout. Also, cooking at a low temperature means you don't have to let the meat rest at the end, so there's no extra time at the end before you can eat it! The addition of Parmesan and herbs on the crust will knock your socks off—literally! So make sure your shoes are on and your laces are really tight! Also, rinse your meat thermometer in ice water before sticking it into the meat. This will reset it and give you a more accurate reading.

One 8- to 12-pound prime rib roast of beef, boned and untied (you don't need to tie your meat all the time—this will make it juicier)

2 cups grated Parmesan cheese

2 tablespoons finely minced fresh rosemary

2 tablespoons finely minced fresh sage

2 tablespoons finely minced fresh thyme

1 tablespoon kosher salt and 1 tablespoon freshly ground black pepper

2 tablespoons finely minced garlic

½ cup olive oil

Preheat the oven to 225°F. Heat a heavy skillet, Dutch oven, or flame-proof roasting pan large enough to accommodate the roast over high fire. Sear the roast on all sides in the dry pan, until it is nicely browned and crunchy, about 10 minutes per side.

Remove the pan from heat and let the meat rest until cool enough to handle. While it is resting, combine the Parmesan, rosemary, sage, thyme, salt, pepper, and garlic in a bowl.

Coat the roast with the olive oil, then press the herb mixture over the meat, making sure that all sides of the roast are coated. Transfer the roast to a large roasting pan, and roast until the internal temperature reaches 122°F for rare, 132° to 134°F for medium-rare, or 145°F for medium, roughly 3½ hours.

Turn off the oven and leave the roast for about 20 minutes. Transfer the roast to a platter and serve.

— {Continued} —

Yorkshire Puddings

A *must* side dish for anything that features gravy or pan juices. When you have something fatty, oily, and tasty with gravy, like pot roast or a piece of braised meat, Yorkshire puddings are the very best way to soak up all the liquid. A dear friend of mine in Moorpark, Maureen, does the best one you'll ever have in your life, and she taught me how to do it.

⅔ cup plus 2 tablespoons flour
½ teaspoon kosher salt
½ teaspoon ground white pepper
2 whole eggs plus 2 egg yolks, lightly beaten
1 cup milk
¼ cup roast drippings or melted butter

In a medium bowl, whisk together the flour, salt, and pepper. Add the eggs, egg yolks, and milk, whisking until the batter is well mixed. Let the batter rest for 30 minutes.

Preheat the oven to 450°F. Spoon 1 teaspoon of the melted fat or butter on the bottom of each cup of a popover pan and place in the oven for 5 minutes to preheat.

Mix the batter a bit more and pour into a pitcher or carafe. Pour it into the hot pan as soon as you remove it from the oven, filling up each cup a little more than halfway.

Return the pan to the oven and bake for 15 minutes. Reduce the heat to 350°F and continue baking until the puddings are browned, 15 to 20 minutes. (The less you open the oven door, the better, so try to resist!)

When they are done, tip the puddings out of the pan, poke each one with a skewer to let the steam out so they don't collapse, and let them cool for a few minutes on a rack before serving.

Beef and Wine Stew with Black Olives

2½ pounds beef round, cut
    into 1½-inch cubes

¼ cup flour

8 tablespoons (1 stick) butter

2 tablespoons extra-virgin
    olive oil

¼ cup Marsala

1½ cups red wine

½ cup beef stock

1 bay leaf

Kosher salt and freshly ground
    black pepper

5 to 6 sprigs fresh thyme tied
    with twine

One 1-inch-long strip of
    orange peel

1 cup button or cremini
    mushrooms, halved

1 garlic clove, crushed

1 cup pitted black olives

½ cup chopped fresh flat-leaf
    parsley

Lighting the Marsala wine on fire while preparing this dish is fun, sure, but it also has a purpose. The flame takes the strength of the alcohol away, but leaves the sauce with a nice sweet finish.

Dust the beef with the flour.

Melt the butter with the oil in a Dutch oven over medium-high heat. Add the meat and brown it until the outer red color is gone, which can take anywhere from 10 to 20 minutes. Keep an eye on it!

Increase the heat to high, add the Marsala and, with the help of a long match, set the alcohol aflame and let it burn out.

Add the red wine and let it bubble fast for about half a minute. Add stock and bay leaf. Season with a dash of salt and pepper and add the bouquet of thyme and orange peel with the mushrooms and garlic. Turn the flame as low as possible, cover the pan with at least 3 layers of parchment paper, and then place the lid over it.

Cook the stew for about 3 hours. Five minutes before serving, remove the thyme bouquet and add the pitted black olives. Taste for seasoning, add parsley for color, and serve with crusty bread or boiled rice.

Braised Beef Brisket with Onions and Balsamic Reduction

SERVES 4 TO 6

I often put slices of this meat between two pieces of grilled bread for the best "clean" sloppy Joe you'll ever have.

Preheat the oven to 320°F. In a small bowl, combine the salt and pepper, paprika, garlic powder, onion powder, and chili powder. Set aside.

Heat the olive oil in a large Dutch oven over medium-high heat. Add the onions and garlic and cook until soft and light brown, about 10 minutes. Remove from the heat.

Rub the meat on all sides with the adobo sauce, then coat it with the seasoning mix and place it in the Dutch oven with the fattiest side down.

In a small bowl, whisk together the ketchup, reduced balsamic vinegar, molasses, and water and pour the mixture over the brisket. Place the lid on the Dutch oven and put it into the oven.

Braise the meat until it is very tender, about 3 hours. Remove from the oven, and transfer the meat to a cutting board. Skim the fat off the pan sauce and set aside. Slice the meat and serve with the sauce.

2 teaspoons kosher salt

1 teaspoon freshly ground black pepper

1 teaspoon paprika

1 teaspoon garlic powder

1 teaspoon onion powder

1 teaspoon chili powder

3 tablespoons olive oil

3 medium red onions, sliced into thick rounds

5 garlic cloves, peeled and crushed

One 4-pound beef brisket, untrimmed

2 tablespoons adobo sauce from a can of chipotle peppers in adobo sauce

1 cup ketchup

½ cup balsamic vinegar reduced (recipe follows)

½ cup dark molasses

⅔ cup water

Balsamic Vinegar Reduction

In a saucepan, bring the vinegar to boil, reduce the heat, and simmer for 8 to 10 minutes until the vinegar has thickened and starts to smell like caramel.

Remove from the heat, cool completely, then whisk in corn syrup.

3 cups balsamic vinegar

½ cup light corn syrup

SERVES 4

Old-time
Chicken Fried Steak

2 eggs

Kosher salt and freshly ground
    black pepper

1 cup plus 1 teaspoon flour

1 teaspoon smoked paprika

2 cups dry bread crumbs

Four 3-ounce beef round,
    shoulder, or chuck steaks,
    about ¼ inch thick

¼ cup light olive oil

2 cups milk

½ cup crumbled cooked sweet
    Italian sausage

This is a classic, so you need to use a classic cooking utensil to make it: a cast-iron skillet. People believe that the seasoning of the cast iron infuses the food with a special aroma. Personally, I think that's a tasty lie, but it's okay because cast iron will hold the heat perfectly and keep it consistent, which is really why it's a go-to pan for frying.

Preheat the oven to 250°F.

In a shallow bowl, lightly beat the eggs and season with salt and pepper. In another shallow bowl, combine 1 cup of the flour with the paprika, and season it with salt and pepper as well. Place the bread crumbs in a third shallow bowl.

Pat the steaks dry with paper towels and season both sides with salt and pepper. Dredge each steak first in the flour mixture, then the egg, allowing the excess to drip off, and then dredge in bread crumbs. Set the steaks aside on a plate.

Heat the olive oil in a cast-iron skillet over medium-high heat. Add the steaks, working in batches if necessary, and cook until they have a golden crust, about 4 minutes per side. Transfer to a baking sheet and place in oven to keep warm.

Pour off all but about 2 tablespoons of the oil from the skillet. Add the remaining 1 teaspoon flour and cook over low heat, whisking, until golden, about 30 seconds. Whisking constantly, slowly add the milk and then the sausage. Raise the heat to medium-high and boil until the gravy has thickened, about 5 minutes. Season with salt and pepper, pour over the steaks, and serve immediately.

Hamburgers

This recipe makes burgers cooked medium. If you like them a little rarer or a little more well-done, just adjust the cooking time by a minute or two in either direction. If you don't see ground short rib at your butcher, ask them to grind it for you.

In a large bowl, combine the ground beef and ground short rib meat and mix well.

Form three equal-sized burger patties. Season each side of the burgers with salt and pepper to taste.

Heat olive oil on grill pan, then start to cook the burgers. They will need to cook for a total of 3 or 4 minutes per each side.

In a separate spot on the grill pan, grill the onion slices until they are caramelized.

When the burgers are almost done, place a slice of cheese on each patty to allow the cheese to melt.

Once they are cooked, remove the burgers from the pan and set aside and let rest for 2 minutes so the juice will redistribute into the meat.

While the burgers rest, grill the rolls, facedown, on the same grill until toasted on each side. This will only take a few minutes.

Spread a little mayo on the bread, top with the burger, tomato slices, and lettuce and finish with ketchup.

1 pound ground beef

8 ounces ground short rib meat

Kosher salt and freshly ground black pepper

Olive oil, for the pan

1 large red onion sliced

3 slices cheddar cheese

3 potato burger buns

3 tablespoons mayonnaise

1 large tomato, cut into thick slices

1 head butter lettuce

3 tablespoons ketchup

Variations:

Instead of potato buns, use pretzel buns

Instead of cheddar cheese, use provolone

Instead of red onion, use caramelized balsamic onion (recipe follows)

— {Continued} —

Balsamic Onions

Place a large sauté pan over high heat. Once it just begins to smoke, turn off the heat, add the oil and then add the onions. Place the pan back on medium-high heat, and cook the onions, stirring only occasionally, until caramelized, 8 to 10 minutes. Season with salt and pepper.

Add the vinegar and reduce until it has somewhat thickened. Remove the pan from the heat, add the corn syrup and stir well. Let the onions cool in the pan. Season to taste.

2 tablespoons olive oil

3 medium onions, halved and cut into thin slices

Kosher salt and freshly ground black pepper

½ cup balsamic vinegar

1 tablespoon light corn syrup

Whole Beef Tenderloin, Peppered and Grilled

2 tablespoons ground white pepper

2 tablespoons freshly ground black pepper

2 tablespoons red or pink peppercorns

2 tablespoons garlic powder

¼ cup extra-virgin olive oil

2 tablespoons chipotle paste

Kosher salt

One 6- to 7-pound whole beef tenderloin, trimmed and tied

A simple way to impress, this is easy to make, and can also be cooked 100 percent in the oven during wintertime or when you don't have a grill handy.

In a bowl, combine the white pepper, black pepper, pink peppercorns, garlic powder, olive oil, chipotle paste, and salt and, using either a brush or your hands (which is what my family prefers), massage and coat the meat with the mixture.

Prepare a medium-hot fire on the grill or heat a flat top on your stovetop that is big enough to fit the whole loin.

Preheat the oven to 325°F.

Grill the meat over the hottest part of the grill or flat top, turning it as a good brown crust develops. Grilling time will vary depending on your grill and the heat. When the meat is browned all over, stick a thermometer in and put it in the oven to cook until the internal temperature reaches 120°F for rare or 130°F for medium-rare. Start checking the temperature after the first 10 minutes to make sure you don't overcook it.

Remove the meat from the oven and let it rest for 15 minutes. Slice and serve.

Rolled Flank Steak with Mint Pesto

SERVES 6

This dish elevates the classic grilled steak to the next level, and the pesto inside makes the steak super moist and the presentation very dramatic.

Place the flank steak flat on a work surface with the grain of the meat running perpendicular to you. Using a long, thin, very sharp knife, butterfly the meat by slicing through the long side of the steak, opening it up as you go, stopping ½ inch short of cutting the steak in two.

Season with salt and pepper.

Spread the pesto all over the meat, leaving a 1½-inch space all around the edge. Roll up the steak, with the grain running the length of the roll, and tie up with kitchen string every 2 inches. Wrap with plastic wrap and refrigerate until ready to cook.

Preheat the oven to 350°F. Rub the steak with olive oil, then sear it in a very hot cast-iron skillet over high heat or on a very hot grill. Place it in the oven for 15 to 20 minutes for medium-rare steak.

Place the steak on a cutting board and allow it to rest for 10 minutes. Remove the strings and carve across the grain into 1- to 2-inch slices.

One 3-pound flank steak
Kosher salt and freshly ground black pepper
2 cups fresh mint pesto (see page 40; simply replace the basil with half mint and half baby spinach)
2 tablespoons olive oil

ON THE SIDE

Veggies and Other Accompaniments

GREEN. RED. PURPLE. YELLOW. ORANGE. I COULD LIST ALL THE
colors of the rainbow, mix some colors together, and still probably have some color combos that hadn't been touched on. It's vegetable time people. You know, that little side next to your meat? The stuff that's always eaten last because it's mushy and tastes bad? With so much color, taste, and variety, why would you *not* want to have some? It's my mission to show you fun, flavorful, and delicious ways to cook and eat your veggies, whether you're a vegetarian, vegan, or carnivore.

When I was a kid, vegetables were always on the table. Grandpa and Grandma grew our food in the backyard. If they grew it, we ate it. Carrots, garden peas, and potatoes were always on the table. So unlike most American kids who are exposed to vegetables, but only after a fast-food hamburger, I thought that eating veggies was what everyone did. I had no idea that I was in the small percentage of children that actually enjoyed vegetables! I was excited to see the different ways to prepare a potato, how green beans had so much snap, and that greens cooked in a rich beef stock made the best soups. I wasn't thinking about my health, but looking back, it looks like my family was greatly interested in it. So thanks to my family for always putting them on my plate.

Vegetables are probably the side of choice when it comes to lunch and dinner. A typical dinner plate consists of protein, starch, and vegetables, in that order. If you aren't a loyal vegetarian, chances are that you aren't eating enough vegetables; in fact, as many as 75 percent of Americans are not receiving proper amounts of them. Let's change that! How about Brussels sprouts? Probably not your first choice in the veggie world right? That's because you've probably had them once, they were mushy and underseasoned, and you thought, "Never again." This too often is what I hear from my friends. It's not the vegetables' fault that you don't know what to do with them. Thankfully they are forgiving and would love for you to give them another chance. Use a garlic oil, caramelize heavily, deglaze with balsamic vinegar, and end with a touch of Worcestershire sauce. Time to eat!

Braised Collard Greens with Beans, Peperoncino, and Pancetta

SERVES 4

This is great in chillier months when collards are at their peak. You can also use cabbage, Swiss chard, or kale in this recipe.

Prepare an ice bath by filling a large bowl with ice and cold water. Set aside.

Bring a large pot of water to a boil, add the collard greens, and blanch for 2 to 3 minutes. Drain and immediately plunge them into the ice bath to stop them from cooking further. Remove from the ice bath, drain, and set aside.

Heat the oil in a deep sauté pan over medium heat, add the onions, garlic, and red pepper flakes and cook until the onions begin to soften, about 3 minutes. Season with salt and black pepper, raise the heat to medium, and continue to cook until the onions have caramelized, another 5 minutes or so.

Add the pancetta and cook for about 5 minutes, or until it has started to crisp. Add the collard greens, and stir together for a few minutes to combine the flavors, then add the stock. Bring to a simmer, cover partially, and simmer over low heat for about 45 minutes more. Add the beans and the lemon juice and cook for another 10 minutes on low heat.

Serve really hot.

2 pounds collard greens, stems removed and roughly chopped

3 tablespoons extra-virgin olive oil

2 red onions, sliced in half and then very thin

5 garlic cloves, minced

1 teaspoon crushed red pepper flakes (peperoncino)

Kosher salt and freshly ground black pepper

6 ounces chopped pancetta

1 cup vegetable stock

15 ounces canned cannellini beans, rinsed and drained

Juice of 1 lemon

Sautéed Spinach

SERVES 6

This is such a nice, simple dish. All you need is a drizzle of olive oil, some crushed garlic, and a good handful of spinach. I suggest using baby spinach, which cooks fast and stays super-moist, but if you like more texture you can use grown-up spinach. This dish is perfect with the Skirt Steak with Oven Fries on page 143.

Melt the butter with the oil in a large pot over medium heat. Once the butter has turned a little bit brown, 5 to 7 minutes, add the garlic and shallot and cook until softened, about 3 minutes. Add the spinach all at once, turning it with tongs to coat it evenly. When it starts to wilt, transfer the spinach from the heat to a colander and drain any excess liquid.

This spinach is delicious at room temperature, so you can set it aside until the rest of your meal is ready, then season to your taste with salt and pepper and serve.

2 tablespoons butter
2 tablespoons extra-virgin olive oil
4 garlic cloves, crushed
1 small shallot, finely chopped
1½ pounds fresh baby spinach (fresh in a bag is fine)
Kosher salt and freshly ground black pepper

Yellow Squash Casserole

4 yellow squash, ends trimmed
and cut into ½-inch chunks

1 yellow onion, chopped

4 garlic cloves, minced

⅔ cup chicken stock

1½ cups mascarpone cheese

1 teaspoon chopped fresh
thyme

Kosher salt and freshly ground
black pepper

1 cup panko bread crumbs
mixed with ½ cup Parme-
san cheese and 2 teaspoons
garlic powder

2 tablespoons extra-virgin
olive oil

A simple, delicious dish. The slow cooking process brings out all the sweetness of the squash.

Position a rack in the center of the oven and preheat the oven to 350°F. Butter a baking dish large enough to hold all the vegetables.

Bring the squash, onion, garlic, and stock to a boil in a saucepan. Cook until all the broth is gone. Stir in the mascarpone and thyme and season to taste with salt and pepper. Spread out the vegetable mixture in the prepared baking dish. Sprinkle with bread crumbs and drizzle with the oil.

Bake the casserole until the juices are simmering and the top is crusty, about 30 minutes. Let stand for 5 minutes, then serve hot.

Grilled Green Tomatoes with Feta, Mint, and Basil

6 large green tomatoes

¼ cup extra-virgin olive oil

Kosher salt and freshly ground black pepper

1 teaspoon garlic powder

6 ounces feta cheese

30 fresh mint leaves

Chopped fresh basil, for garnish

2 tablespoons balsamic vinegar

This is the best way to salvage unripe tomatoes that have fallen on the ground in your garden or made it into the store before ripening—savory and not too sweet!

Slice the tomatoes into ½-inch-thick rounds and put them in a bowl with 2 tablespoons of the olive oil, salt and pepper to taste, and the garlic powder. Toss together until they are all nicely coated.

Heat a grill or a flat top on your stove to a very high heat, and grill the tomatoes on both sides until they start to char and caramelize.

Transfer the tomatoes to a platter and crumble the feta cheese on top of them. Garnish with the mint leaves and basil, then drizzle with the remaining 2 tablespoons olive oil and the balsamic vinegar.

Creamed Corn and Mozzarella

I had this dish in Texas made creamy with cheddar cheese. Once I tried it with mozzarella and I've never gone back. I make it in a slow cooker, but if you want to do it on the stovetop it will take about 30-45 minutes.

8 cups fresh corn kernels (drained canned corn is also OK)
½ cup heavy cream
6 ounces cream cheese, torn into chunks
3 tablespoons butter
2 tablespoons sugar
6 ounces mozzarella cheese, torn into chunks
Kosher salt and freshly ground black pepper

Place 1½ cups of the corn kernels in a blender with the cream and purée until smooth.

Put the corn purée, cream cheese, butter, and sugar into a slow cooker. Cover and cook on high for 1½ hours.

Add the remaining corn kernels and the mozzarella and cook, stirring for about 5 minutes to incorporate them. Season with salt and pepper and serve.

Roasted Potatoes in Tomato Sauce

3 pounds russet potatoes, cut
    into 1½-inch pieces
¼ cup olive oil
Kosher salt and freshly ground
    black pepper
1 red onion, chopped
5 garlic cloves, chopped
½ cup red wine
2 tablespoons tomato paste
16 ounces canned crushed
    tomatoes
1 teaspoon kosher salt
1 teaspoon sugar
1 teaspoon smoked paprika

Saucy potatoes are the perfect side dish for a grilled or roasted piece of meat.

Preheat the oven to 375°F. Toss the potatoes with 3 tablespoons of the olive oil and season with salt and pepper. Arrange in one layer in a casserole and roast until the outsides of the potatoes are crisp, 30 to 40 minutes.

Heat the remaining 1 tablespoon olive oil in a pot set over medium heat. Add the onion and garlic and cook until they begin to brown, about 5 minutes.

Add the wine to the pan and increase the heat to high. Reduce the wine by half, then add the tomato paste and stir to combine. Add the crushed tomatoes, salt, sugar, and smoked paprika. Stir well and reduce the heat to low. Let the sauce cook slowly while the potatoes are still in the oven.

When the potatoes are brown and crispy, remove the casserole from the oven and pour the tomato sauce over them. Return the potatoes to the oven and continue to cook until the sauce has become thick, 12 to 15 minutes.

Baby Potatoes Roasted in Parchment Paper

SERVES 6

Serve these on the paper from the bottom of the roasting pan for a terrific presentation.

Preheat the oven to 375°F. Place 2 sheets of parchment paper onto a roasting pan.

In a bowl, toss together the potatoes, mint, rosemary, garlic, salt, pepper, and olive oil, making sure that the potatoes are well coated.

Pour the potatoes onto the parchment paper–covered roasting pan, and cover with 2 more sheets of parchment paper. Fold the edges of the parchment in to seal the potatoes. Cook them in the oven for about 35 minutes, or until they are crispy.

About 30 to 40 baby potatoes (any colors you like)
20 fresh mint leaves
2 tablespoons fresh rosemary
4 garlic cloves, crushed
2 teaspoons kosher salt
2 teaspoons freshly ground black pepper
3 tablespoons olive oil

Roasted Scalloped Potatoes with Creamy Sun-dried Tomato Pesto

SERVES 8

I always find classic scalloped potatoes a bit boring and monotone, so I added sun-dried tomato pesto, which is not only tastier but makes the potatoes an even better pairing with lots of dishes. They go well with the Whole Beef Tenderloin, Peppered and Grilled on page 155.

3 pounds baking potatoes

1 cup sun-dried tomato pesto (recipe follows)

Kosher salt and freshly ground black pepper

2 cups shredded Fontina cheese

3 tablespoons fresh chopped flat-leaf parsley

1 cup heavy cream

Position a rack in the center of the oven and preheat the oven to 425°F. Lightly oil a baking dish large enough to hold the potatoes.

Cut the potatoes into ⅓-inch rounds. Bring a pot of water to a boil, then add the potatoes and cook for about 10 minutes, or until they are barely fork-tender. Drain and toss with the pesto to coat evenly. Season to taste with salt and pepper.

Put one layer potatoes in the baking dish, sprinkle with the Fontina, then put another layer of potatoes on top and another layer of cheese. Continue until you have 3 layers, finishing with cheese. Sprinkle the parsley on top.

Heat the cream in a small pot until just to the boiling point. Pour it over the potatoes then cover the pan tightly with aluminum foil.

Bake for 30 minutes. Halfway through the baking time, lower the oven temperature to 375°F, uncover the pan, and continue to bake until the cheese is bubbling and starting to brown.

Sun-dried Tomato Pesto

In a food processor, blitz the tomatoes, grated cheese, pine nuts, olive oil, basil, parsley, spinach, garlic, and salt and pepper to taste until a paste forms. If needed add a touch of water or oil to thin out to your liking.

2 cups sun-dried tomatoes (page 13)

1 cup grated pecorino Romano cheese

¼ cup pine nuts

2 tablespoons extra-virgin olive oil

½ cup fresh basil leaves

¼ cup flat-leaf parsley (you can keep the tender stalks in if you want, or just use leaves)

¼ cup baby spinach

3 garlic cloves, smashed and peeled

Kosher salt and freshly ground black pepper

Butternut Squash and Potato Salad from the Oven with Herb Dressing

SERVES 6

This is a different, warm take on salad that is great for colder months. But you don't have to serve it hot. You can make it, then let it sit at room temperature (don't put it in the fridge, which will coagulate the oil). Mix it with some greens, like arugula, mache, or baby kale, and you have a great summer salad.

Preheat the oven to 350°F. Line a baking sheet with parchment paper.

Peel the squash using a peeler, then halve each one and scoop out and discard the seeds. Cut all of the squash and potatoes into a medium dice. Place in a large bowl.

Combine the olive oil, garlic, paprika, Parmesan, rosemary, thyme, shallots, salt, pepper, and butter to make a dressing. Mix with squash and potato cubes.

Spread the squash and potato cubes out on the lined baking sheet and bake for 30 minutes until they are al dente and golden brown, turning the pan occasionally and stirring the squash and potatoes when you do so that they brown evenly. Bake another 10 minutes, then transfer to a bowl and serve warm with some rosemary, some Parmesan, and the parsley on top for garnish.

3 butternut squash, about 4½ pounds total

4 medium potatoes, peeled (russets work well)

½ cup olive oil

2 garlic cloves, crushed

2 teaspoons ground smoked paprika

½ cup grated Parmesan cheese, plus extra for garnish

1 bunch fresh rosemary, minced (save some leaves for the garnish)

1 tablespoon minced thyme

1 tablespoon minced shallots

Kosher salt and freshly ground black pepper

8 tablespoons (1 stick) butter, melted

¼ cup chopped fresh flat-leaf parsley

Borlotti Beans with Sautéed Baby Kale and Braised Collard Greens

Borlotti is a big brownish-red bean widely used in Italy. If your store doesn't have them, don't change stores and never show up there again! Instead, make this dish with lima beans or regular brown beans (and keep an eye on the cooking time to make sure they don't get too soft).

Heat the oil in a Dutch oven or deep skillet over low heat. Add the onion and garlic and cook until the garlic starts to caramelize, about 3 minutes.

Cut the kale and the collard greens into 1-inch strips, add them to the pot, and turn the heat up to high. Stirring continuously with a wooden spoon, to make sure the garlic doesn't burn, cook until the greens have wilted and their moisture has released and evaporated, about 10 minutes.

Add the beans and rosemary to the pot and cook for another 5 minutes. Remove the rosemary, add the tomatoes, and season with salt and pepper. With the fire still on high, cook for another 10 minutes. When the tomatoes have reduced remove from heat, let rest for a few minutes, and serve with a nice drizzle of olive oil and some crusty bread.

¼ cup extra-virgin olive oil

1 medium red onion, diced

4 garlic cloves, thinly sliced

2 pounds kale, ribs removed

1 pound collard greens, ribs removed

4 cups cooked and drained borlotti or brown beans

1 rosemary sprig

1 cup crushed canned plum tomatoes

Kosher salt and freshly ground black pepper

Extra-virgin olive oil, for drizzling

SERVES 8

Bean Casserole, Sun-dried Tomatoes and Parmesan Crust

3 tablespoons butter, plus
    more, softened, for the bak-
    ing dish
4½ tablespoons extra-virgin
    olive oil
1 red onion, cut in ¼-inch dice
½ pound sun-dried tomatoes
    (page 13), quartered (if you
    use store-bought sun-dried
    tomatoes packed in oil,
    squeeze out as much oil as
    you can)
¼ cup water
Kosher salt and freshly ground
    black pepper
1 teaspoon fresh thyme
1 tablespoon kosher salt
1 tablespoon baking soda
1½ pounds green beans,
    trimmed and cut in half
¼ cup plus 2 tablespoons flour
2 cups half-and-half
1 cup grated Parmesan cheese
2 teaspoons paprika
½ cup bread crumbs
3 shallots, roughly sliced
1 scallion, thinly sliced

This is my answer to canned fried onion and cheap mushroom soup casserole on Thanksgiving. Please, TRY THIS AT HOME—you won't regret it!

Preheat the oven to 375°F.

In a deep sauté pan, combine 1½ tablespoons of the butter and 1½ tablespoons of the oil over medium heat. Add the onion and sauté, stirring occasionally, until it begins to soften.

Add the sun-dried tomatoes and water and cook, stirring occasionally, until the tomatoes are softened and most of the liquid has evaporated, about 10 minutes. Season with salt, pepper, and thyme and remove from the heat.

Bring a large pot of water to a boil, add the tablespoon of salt and the baking soda (it will preserve the green color of the beans). Add the beans and blanch until just tender, about 5 minutes. Drain and cool them under cold running water.

Add the beans to the sun-dried tomato mix and set aside.

In a saucepan over medium heat, melt the remaining 1½ tablespoons butter and 1½ tablespoons oil and add ¼ cup of the flour. Turn the heat down to low and cook, whisking constantly, until golden brown. Gradually add the half-and-half and continue whisking until the mixture has thickened, about 3 minutes.

Transfer the bean and tomato mix to a casserole or oven dish and pour the half-and-half mixture over it. Combine the Parmesan, paprika, and bread crumbs and sprinkle on top. Cover the casserole with aluminum foil and bake for about 45 minutes, then remove the foil and continue baking until the top is golden brown, about 10 minutes more.

Heat the remaining 1½ tablespoons of olive oil in a medium

skillet over medium-high heat. Toss the shallots with the remaining 2 tablespoons of flour, then fry in batches, turning frequently, until golden brown. Using a slotted spatula, transfer the fried shallots to paper towels to drain.

When the casserole has finished baking, remove it from the oven; top with fried shallots and scallions and let cool slightly before serving.

Skillet Corn Bread

MAKES ONE 8-INCH ROUND CORN BREAD

I never had corn bread until I went to Louisiana and then I got addicted to it. It's good for everything—for an appetizer with butter and honey, for stuffing for your turkey instead of croutons, for a side, or as a dessert. I don't think there's anything from the baking world that is more versatile than corn bread. It also freezes really well, so make a huge batch. Then all you have to do is put it in the oven at a high temp for a few minutes to thaw it, and it tastes like fresh-baked.

Light olive oil, for oiling the pan
1 cup fine yellow cornmeal, preferably stone-ground
¼ cup plus 1 tablespoon flour
⅓ cup plus 1 tablespoon packed light brown sugar
1 teaspoon baking powder
1 teaspoon baking soda
½ teaspoon kosher salt
1 whole egg plus 3 egg yolks
1 cup buttermilk
½ cup milk
3 tablespoons butter, melted and cooled
¼ cup chopped fresh jalapeño peppers, ribs and seeds removed before chopping

Preheat oven to 425°F. Lightly oil an 8-inch cast-iron skillet and place in the oven to preheat.

Whisk together the cornmeal, flour, sugar, baking powder, baking soda, and salt in a large bowl. In a small bowl lightly beat together the egg and egg yolks. In a separate bowl, combine the buttermilk, milk, eggs, and egg yolks. Add this wet mixture to the cornmeal mixture and whisk to combine. Add the butter and jalapeños, and whisk some more to combine it all into a batter. Remove the skillet from the oven and pour in the batter; it will sizzle. Return the skillet to the oven and bake the corn bread until dark golden around the edges and set in center, 25 to 30 minutes. Let cool slightly in the skillet before cutting into squares or wedges.

Homemade Focaccia with Olives, Rosemary, and Sun-dried Tomato

MAKES 1 FOCACCIA, ABOUT 18 × 13 INCHES

This is my everyday bread, flavored with tons of herbs and tomatoes and a sure hit on everyone's table. (Hint: extra olive oil is a MUST!)

In a stand mixer fitted with the hook attachment, combine the flour, water, salt, and yeast and mix for about 12 minutes. The dough should be very pliable and not too wet. Fold in half of the olives, half of the sun-dried tomatoes, and half of the rosemary and mix for another minute.

Place the dough in an oiled bowl, cover with plastic wrap, and set it aside to rise for 1 hour.

Thoroughly oil a half sheet pan or rimmed baking sheet using plenty of olive oil. Punch down the dough then form it into a slab that more or less fits into the baking sheet. Press the dough into the corners of the sheet using your fingers. Do not worry about any unevenness. Cover with the remaining olives, tomatoes, and rosemary and drizzle generously with olive oil. Press everything in place using your fingers.

Lastly, sprinkle some coarse sea salt (if using) on the bread and allow it to rise for another 30 minutes or so.

In the meantime, preheat the oven to 350°F. Bake the focaccia until golden brown, approximately 25 minutes, then let it rest in the oven for another 10 minutes before serving. You can cut the focaccia into squares, or just let everyone tear off pieces—which is more fun!

3½ cups flour

1⅓ cups lukewarm water

Pinch of kosher salt

2 packages (5½ teaspoons) active dry yeast

1½ cups mixed pitted olives, cut into rounds

1 cup sun-dried tomatoes (page 13)

3 tablespoons minced fresh rosemary

Extra-virgin olive oil, for oiling

2 tablespoons coarse sea salt (optional)

No-Knead Bread

3 cups bread flour, plus more
   for dusting

2 teaspoons instant dry yeast

1 teaspoon sugar

1½ cups water plus 1
   tablespoon

1¼ teaspoons kosher salt

Although this bread is very easy and requires little to no work, you still need to find the time to let the dough rest. It needs to rise again so the yeast will be activated.

Using a whisk, mix together 2 cups of the flour, the yeast, and the sugar in a large bowl. Add the water, mix well, and cover with plastic wrap. Let rest for 2 hours. The dough is ready when you see lots of bubbles on the surface.

Add the remaining 1 cup of flour on top of the dough in the bowl and gently fold in with a plastic spatula until the flour is almost all absorbed.

Flour a towel and place the ball on it, let it rest for 45 minutes.

About 15 minutes before the dough is ready, preheat the oven to 450°F and put a cast-iron pot with a lid or a Dutch oven in it to warm up. When the dough is ready, carefully remove the pot from the oven. Slide your hand under the towel and turn the dough over into the pot, bottom side up. Sprinkle salt on top.

Cover the pot with the lid and bake the bread for 30 minutes. Remove the lid and bake until the loaf of bread is beautifully browned, 15 to 30 minutes. Remove the loaf from the pot and let it cool on a wire rack before slicing.

Creamed Corn Muffins

Using a potato masher or a food processor to crush some of the corn gives you more flavor and a creamier texture than leaving the kernels whole. It's worth the extra step.

Preheat the oven to 350°F. Line a standard 12-cup muffin pan with paper liners.

Whisk together the cornmeal, flour, 1 cup of the sugar, the baking powder, and the salt in a large bowl.

In another large bowl, combine the corn, oil, butter, and honey. Lightly beat the eggs with the egg yolks then stir them and 1 cup of the cream into the corn mixture.

Stir the corn mixture into the cornmeal mixture and mix well. Pour into the lined muffin pan, filling each cup about two-thirds of the way full. Place the pan in the oven and bake until the muffin tops are golden and a toothpick inserted into the centers comes out clean, 15 to 20 minutes. For even baking, rotate the pan halfway through the baking time.

In the meantime, combine the remaining 1 cup cream in a small saucepan with the remaining 2 teaspoons sugar and the vanilla and heat over medium-low heat until it is creamy and reduced by half, no longer than 5 minutes.

Let the muffins cool for 5 minutes before turning them out of the pans, then serve them warm with the cream sauce drizzled on top.

1 cup plus 2 tablespoons yellow cornmeal

1 cup flour

1 cup plus 2 teaspoons sugar

2 tablespoons baking powder

1¾ teaspoons kosher salt

½ cup canned corn, drained and crushed

¼ cup neutral-tasting oil, such as light olive oil

4 tablespoons (½ stick) butter, melted

2 tablespoons honey

2 whole eggs plus 2 egg yolks

2 cups heavy cream

1 teaspoon pure vanilla extract

Winter Squash Buns

10 ounces winter squash,
  peeled, in cubes

1 teaspoon paprika

1 teaspoon red curry powder

1 teaspoon freshly grated
  nutmeg

Kosher salt and freshly ground
  black pepper

3 tablespoons butter plus more
  for the baking sheet

1 package (2¼ teaspoons)
  active dry yeast

2¼ cups flour

10 ounces pecorino Romano
  cheese

1 cup milk

This is the next best thing after sliced bread. Use it for your burgers and you won't be disappointed (and if you use smaller molds, you can use it for sliders!).

Preheat the oven to 300°F. Grease a baking sheet with butter.

Arrange the squash on the prepared baking sheet in one layer. Sprinkle with the paprika, curry powder, nutmeg, salt, and pepper.

Roast the squash until done, about 30 minutes. Place it in the fridge for about 30 minutes.

When the squash has cooled, purée it in a food processor with the butter, yeast, flour, and cheese.

Add the milk, little by little, depending on how liquid the mixture is (this depends on how much water the squash has). You may not need all the milk. Continue to combine in the food processor until it forms a slightly sticky dough.

Grease a bowl with oil, place the dough ball in it and cover with plastic wrap. Let it rise for an hour, then remove the dough, knead it once more, and divide it into 12 balls. Let the dough balls rise again for 45 minutes. While you're waiting, preheat the oven to 350°F and grease a 12-cup muffin pan.

Place the balls of dough into the prepared pan and bake until golden brown, approximately 30 minutes.

Breakfast
and Brunch

BEFORE YOU BRUSH YOUR TEETH, PUT ON YOUR CLOTHES, CHECK
your e-mails, or anything else you think is important in the morning, you think food. You aren't alone in this matter. As soon as I open my eyes, I crave breakfast. It's like I dream about it to prepare myself for the satisfaction that I'll receive in the morning. Whether I'm relaxing in bed with a bowl of cereal and fruit or doing it up big with eggs, bacon, and biscuits, my mornings always start off the right way.

When I moved to this country, I was overwhelmed by how much you guys celebrate the gathering and partaking of your first meal. I knew if I was going to fully integrate into America, I had to become one with the art of making breakfast. I was no stranger to the concept of breakfast, but for me it was coffee, maybe a pastry and I was off to start my day. Now I've changed my mind and learned how to make tons of delicious breakfast and brunch options.

Because I can see that look on your face as you're reading this. "Fabio, I don't want to get up in the morning at all. Is there any hope for my eating activities?" To which I'll answer in two parts. As far as getting up in the morning, you are on your own on that one. I suggest a dog licking you in the face—kinda messy but usually gets the job done. For your eating activities, there's a secret meal after breakfast and before lunch called Brunch—genius thinking on the name right? Brunch is taking breakfast, adding a pound of butter, and never apologizing. I'm just kidding guys, it's only half a pound.

Brunch allows you to eat like it's breakfast, while still being able to get dressed for the day. No pajamas allowed here people—this is business time. Sometimes brunch even goes all the way until 3 PM on Sundays, which by the way, all depends on how many mimosas are being consumed. Big spreads of muffins, croissants, finger sandwiches, and smoked salmon with the works; brunch to me is always filled with lots of variety in flavors and smells.

So whether you side with breakfast and eat in your underwear, or go with brunch and slip into jeans or a dress, you will be good no matter what! There's something about connecting with food first thing in the morning. Opening your senses up to rich aromas in the comfort of your house is a recipe for a great day. I wouldn't want you missing out on the best way to start your day, so pull down the frying pan, pour some milk, and get your day started with some of these ideas.

Eggs Benedict with Pancetta and Sun-dried Tomatoes

SERVES 8

The tomatoes cut through the richness of the hollandaise sauce here for balance.

MAKE THE SAUCE: Bring a large pot of water to a boil. In a metal bowl that fits over the pot, using a handheld mixer, beat the egg yolks with the water and lemon juice. Sit the bowl on top of the pot of boiling water (the bottom should not touch the water), and lower the heat so the water simmers. Begin whisking the mixture. In 5 to 10 minutes it will lighten and thicken considerably to a firm, foamy consistency.

Begin adding the butter in a thin stream. The magic will happen and the sauce will start to get denser and more creamy by the second. If it is too thick, you can dilute it by adding a few drops of hot water. Remove the bowl from the pan, add the scallions, add Tabasco sauce to taste, and cover with a lid or plate.

PREPARE THE EGGS BENEDICT: Bring a second pot of water to a boil with a splash of vinegar. Lower the heat and keep the water near boiling. Stir in a circular motion to create a vortex. Crack an egg into the center of the vortex and poach for 2 to 3 minutes. Remove the egg from the pan using a slotted spoon and place on a plate lined with paper towels. Repeat with the remaining eggs and set aside in a warm place.

Halve the croissants or rolls and toast to your liking. While they are toasting, pan-fry your ham or pork belly. Place 1 slice of meat on the bottom half of each croissant or roll, then top with a poached egg, and generously cover with hollandaise sauce. Top with a sun-dried tomato, then the other half of the roll or croissant and serve immediately.

Hollandaise Sauce
3 egg yolks
2 tablespoons water
2 tablespoons fresh lemon juice
½ pound (2 sticks) butter, melted and kept warm in a small saucepan
2 scallions, finely chopped
3 dashes Tabasco sauce

Poached Eggs
Dash of vinegar for the water (either red or white wine is fine)
8 eggs, as fresh as possible
8 croissants or other thick, round toasted buns
8 slices ham, or even pork belly slab (recipe follows)
8 sun-dried tomatoes (page 13)

Pork Belly Slab

One 2-pound piece of pork
  belly, scored
10 garlic cloves, minced
2 tablespoons fresh thyme
  leaves
2 tablespoons Dijon mustard
2 teaspoons chopped fresh
  rosemary
1 teaspoon freshly ground
  black pepper

Preheat the oven to 325°F.

Place the pork belly on a cutting board. Mix the remaining ingredients in a bowl and combine completely.

Rub the mixture all over the pork. Place pork on a wire rack set on a baking pan. Cover with aluminum foil and bake for 2 hours.

Remove and let cool completely. Cut into portions and reheat in a skillet over high heat, skin side down, for an unbelievable crispy texture.

Poached Eggs with Espresso-Glazed Bacon

SERVES 4

When you make this, make sure to let the bacon sit on the rack for a few minutes after drizzling it so that all the gooey coffee goodness really sticks to it. When it's done, you can also dip it one more time into the glaze that has dripped into the bottom of the pan.

Serve with Fabio's poached eggs (see recipe page 192).

3 tablespoons brown sugar
1 tablespoon pure maple syrup
¼ cup instant espresso
Pinch of freshly ground black pepper
3 tablespoons water
12 slices thick-cut bacon, smoked if you have it

Preheat the oven to 325°F.

Combine the brown sugar, maple syrup, espresso, and pepper with the water in a pot over low heat. Cook until the sugar begins to caramelize, then remove from heat.

Lay a rack large enough to hold all the bacon on a rimmed baking sheet.

Dip the bacon slices carefully into the espresso syrup, then set them on the rack and drizzle with half of the remaining syrup. Bake for 20 minutes, then pull from the oven and flip the bacon strips. Drizzle the opposite sides of the bacon with the rest of the syrup, then return to the oven for another 15 minutes.

Open-Faced Zucchini Omelet

3 tablespoons extra-virgin
olive oil

8 small zucchini, sliced into
thin rounds

½ small fresh red chile, thinly
sliced

1 garlic clove, finely chopped

8 zucchini flowers, if available

4 eggs

Kosher salt and freshly ground
black pepper

1 tablespoon mascarpone
cheese

Fresh basil leaves, for garnish

For extra flavor, sauté the zucchini with the garlic a little bit longer.

Heat 2 tablespoons of the oil in a sauté pan over medium-high heat.

Add the zucchini and chile and cook until browned, about 5 minutes. Then add the garlic and zucchini flowers if you have them and cook for another 2 minutes. Remove from the pan and set aside.

Heat the remaining 1 tablespoon oil in the pan over medium heat.

Lightly beat the eggs in a small bowl with a pinch of salt and pepper, then mix in the mascarpone.

Pour the eggs into the hot skillet. Add the zucchini mixture before it starts to set.

Cook, allowing the eggs to set slightly in the skillet, breaking them here and there with a spoon to allow the top of the eggs to touch the bottom of the pan. Cover and cook until all the eggs are done, 5 to 10 minutes. The surface of the omelet should feel firm to the touch.

Garnish with the fresh basil and serve.

Frittata with Mint, Spinach, Pecorino, and Cream

SERVES 8

A super tasty, easy way to make breakfast eggs special. If you're fast, you can even shower while it cooks.

Preheat the oven to 350°F. Oil a 9-inch cake pan and line the bottom with parchment paper.

Heat a tablespoon of the olive oil in a sauté pan over medium high heat and add the spinach. Season with salt and pepper and cook, stirring, until the water has released from the spinach and evaporated. Set aside.

Beat the eggs with the cream, mascarpone, and pecorino Romano. Season with salt and pepper.

Combine the spinach with the egg mixture and pour into the prepared pan. Bake the frittata in the middle of the oven for about 15 minutes. It is ready as soon as it feels firm to the touch of a finger.

Remove the pan from the oven. Distribute the mozzarella, mint, and tomatoes evenly over the top, and drizzle with the remaining 3 tablespoons olive oil before serving.

¼ cup extra-virgin olive oil

1 pound spinach, washed, stems removed, and roughly chopped

Kosher salt and freshly ground black pepper

8 eggs

½ cup heavy cream

¼ cup mascarpone cheese (approximately)

½ cup grated pecorino Romano cheese (approximately)

⅓ cup chopped mozzarella cheese, preferably fresh, or packed in water rather than dry

20 to 25 fresh mint leaves

15 cherry tomatoes, halved

Parmesan Biscuits and Sausage Gravy

3 cups flour, plus additional
  for dusting
2 teaspoons baking powder
⅓ cup confectioners' sugar
1 cup grated Parmesan cheese
Pinch of kosher salt
8 tablespoons (1 stick) cold
  butter, cubed
⅔ cup milk or buttermilk, plus
  more for brushing
Freshly ground black pepper
1 recipe Italian Sausage Gravy
  (recipe follows)

This is the single dish that I eat the most for breakfast. If you replace the Parmesan with pecorino Romano, you'll get a stronger flavor.

Preheat the oven to 400°F. Grease or line a baking sheet with parchment paper.

Place the flour, baking powder, sugar, Parmesan, salt, and butter in a food processor or large bowl. Add the milk and work the mixture into a smooth ball (you might need a bit more milk or a bit less, depending how moist the grated cheese is). If using a processor, pulse until everything is combined. If using a bowl, a fork or whisk will do the job.

Dust the countertop with flour. Roll out the ball of dough into a ¾-inch-thick slab. Cut out the biscuits, using a cutter or drinking glass. Continue until all the dough is used up. Brush milk over the biscuits, place them on the prepared baking sheet, and grind a good amount of fresh black pepper on the biscuit tops.

Bake until golden brown, about 15 minutes, depending on size.

— {Continued} —

Italian Sausage Gravy

Cook the sausage in a pan over medium-high heat until it starts to brown, 5 to 7 minutes. When it is almost fully cooked and almost no pink color is left, add the butter and let it melt.

Still over medium-high heat, stir in the flour and keep stirring until there are no lumps. Pour in the milk and the cream slowly, whisking constantly to prevent lumps. Keep cooking until gravy starts to thicken, 4 to 6 minutes (make sure you watch it the whole time so it doesn't boil).

Once it is cooked, add the red pepper flakes if using and stir to combine well. To serve, place a biscuit on each plate and smother it with delicious gravy! You can slice it in half if you want.

1 pound sweet Italian sausage meat, removed from casing and broken into small pieces

6 tablespoons (¾ stick) butter

½ cup flour

2 cups milk

½ cup heavy cream

½ teaspoon crushed red pepper flakes (optional)

Ham, Cheese, and Fried Egg Sandwich

4 tablespoons (½ stick) butter, softened
8 slices bakery white bread
⅓ cup grated Parmesan cheese
8 thin slices ham
8 slices Fontina cheese
2 tablespoons Dijon mustard
4 eggs
¼ cup extra-virgin olive oil

Fried or sunny side up is the best way to make the eggs for these. I personally like sunny side up best because I like the yolk to run all over my sandwich, but for a less messy eater make eggs over easy.

Preheat the oven to 275°F.

Butter 4 slices of the bread and sprinkle with the Parmesan. Top each one with 2 slices each of ham and Fontina and place another slice of bread on top. Transfer the sandwiches to a baking sheet and bake for 3 to 4 minutes. When you see that the cheese has melted and the bread has started to get crusty, take them out and spread 1½ teaspoons of mustard on top of each one.

Fry the eggs in the oil (I like to do this, cooking no more than two at a time, so the whites don't run together). While they are still hot, place one egg on top of each sandwich. Serve the sandwiches with fork and knife.

Sweet Potato and Walnut Waffles

So sweet and crunchy that if you cook them a minute longer, you can make an ice cream sandwich between two of them.

Heat a waffle iron and spray with nonstick cooking spray.

Whisk the flour, sugar, baking powder, cinnamon, and salt in a large bowl. Whisk the half-and-half, sweet potato purée, melted butter, and egg yolks in a separate bowl until well combined and pour into first bowl with the dry ingredients. Whisk just until smooth; do not overmix, but yes you can use a hand mixer if you want.

In a third bowl, beat the egg whites to medium stiff peaks with the hand mixer. Stir one-fourth of the whites into the batter to lighten it, and then fold in the rest. Fold in the walnuts except for those reserved for garnish.

Using a ½-cup scoop, pour batter onto the waffle iron and cook until golden brown. Serve with blueberries, syrup, and some extra chopped walnuts on top.

1½ cups flour

⅓ cup packed brown sugar

2 tablespoons baking powder

1 teaspoon ground cinnamon

½ teaspoon kosher salt

1½ cups half-and-half

½ cup sweet potato purée or canned pure pumpkin purée (*not* pumpkin pie filling)

4 tablespoons (½ stick) butter, melted

3 eggs, separated, at room temperature

½ cup finely chopped walnuts plus 2 tablespoons for garnish

1 cup blueberries

Pure maple syrup, as you like

Squash Flapjacks with Basil Cream

Basil Cream

⅔ cup sour cream

¼ cup chopped fresh basil leaves, blanched and shocked (see head note)

Kosher salt and freshly ground black pepper

1 tablespoon cold water

½ garlic clove

Flapjacks

1 butternut squash, peeled and seeded

3 egg whites

Kosher salt

2 tablespoons cornstarch

Freshly ground black pepper

¼ cup olive oil

½ cup coarsely grated Parmesan cheese, for garnish

To keep your sauce a really bright green, blanch your basil first by immersing it in boiling water for just 30 seconds, then fishing it out with a spider ladle or slotted spoon and shocking it in ice water for a few minutes. This will prevent the chlorophyll in the leaves from turning dark in color. For extra insurance, add ½ teaspoon of baking soda to your boiling water.

Preheat the oven to 400°F.

MAKE THE BASIL CREAM: Blend the sour cream, basil, salt, pepper, water, and garlic in a food processor until smooth. Place in a serving bowl and set aside.

MAKE THE FLAPJACKS: Grate the squash using a coarse grater, place in a baking pan, and roast for 10 minutes. Remove from the oven and let cool. Transfer the squash to a large bowl.

In a separate large bowl, beat the egg whites and a dash of salt with a handheld mixer until stiff peaks form.

Add the cornstarch to the squash and mix well. Generously grind pepper on the mixture. Carefully fold in the beaten egg whites.

Heat a thin layer of oil in a nonstick skillet. Using two tablespoons, drop heaps of the squash mixture onto the hot oil and, using the back of a spoon, press the flapjacks to make them a little flatter. Cook for about 3 minutes, then flip and cook for the same amount of time on the opposite sides.

Drain on paper towels and continue to fry until all the squash mixture has been used.

Serve the flapjacks on a large plate smothered in sauce and the grated Parmesan.

Blueberry and Ricotta Pancakes

The ricotta adds so much creaminess it may make you forget you need syrup. Try some different kinds of berries and have fun with it!

In a bowl, sift together the flour, sugar, baking powder, and salt.

In another bowl, whisk the buttermilk, cream, eggs, vanilla, 1 tablespoon melted butter, and 2 tablespoons of the oil to combine, then whisk into flour mixture. Fold in blueberries.

Heat about 2 teaspoons of softened butter in a large nonstick skillet over medium heat. Using a ladle, pour half cups of batter into the pan. Cook the pancakes until small bubbles form on the surface, about 3 minutes. Before flipping, use a teaspoon to add small dabs of ricotta to each pancake. Cook until the undersides are golden brown and the ricotta has started to brown a bit, about another 3 minutes. Continue frying, adding more butter as needed between batches. Garnish with additional blueberries.

1¾ cups flour

3 tablespoons brown sugar

1 tablespoon baking powder

½ teaspoon kosher salt

1 cup buttermilk

½ cup heavy cream

3 eggs, at room temperature

1 teaspoon pure vanilla extract

1 tablespoon butter, melted, plus more, softened, for the skillet and serving

3 tablespoons extra-light olive oil

1½ cups fresh blueberries, plus more for garnish

1 cup ricotta cheese

Pure maple syrup, for serving

Parmesan-Bacon Grits

2 cups heavy cream

2 cups water

2 teaspoons chopped garlic

1 teaspoon kosher salt

1 cup grits

2 tablespoons butter

1 cup grated Parmesan cheese, plus extra for serving

8 slices bacon, cooked and crumbled

15 sun-dried tomatoes (page 13) cut in half (if you use store-bought sun-dried tomatoes packed in oil, squeeze out as much oil as you can)

4 scallions, chopped, for garnish

For more pungent flavor try adding some diced salami while you're cooking the bacon.

Combine the cream, water, garlic, and salt in a saucepan over medium heat and bring to a simmer. Stir in the grits and continue simmering until they are tender, 30 to 40 minutes.

Stir in the butter and cook until it has melted completely. Then add the Parmesan and the bacon crumbles. Stir to combine and remove from the heat.

Add the sun-dried tomato halves, stir to combine, and serve topped with scallions and more Parmesan.

Buttermilk and
Black Pepper Biscuits

America loves biscuits. I love them with gravy, I love them without. I love biscuits with savory ingredients like roasted ham and sun-dried tomatoes on them. But when you add a lot of black pepper to the biscuits, that's really taking it to the next level. This is a very simple recipe, perfect for the morning.

Preheat the oven to 450°F. Butter a baking sheet.

Sift together the flour, baking powder, sugar, salt, baking soda, Parmesan, and pepper into a bowl.

Work in the butter with your fingers, or pulse in a food processor, until the mixture resembles coarse meal. Mix in buttermilk until just combined.

Turn out the dough onto a lightly floured surface and pat into a 7-inch disk about 1 inch thick. Cut out 12 rounds with a floured 2-inch biscuit cutter, collecting and reshaping the scraps as necessary.

Arrange the biscuits on the buttered baking sheet. Bake until cooked through and golden brown, 10 to 15 minutes, rotating sheet halfway through.

2¼ cups flour, plus more for dusting
2¼ teaspoons baking powder
2 teaspoons sugar
1 teaspoon kosher salt
½ teaspoon baking soda
¼ cup grated Parmesan cheese
3 teaspoons freshly ground black pepper
6 tablespoons (¾ stick) cold butter, cut into small pieces
1 cup buttermilk

Chocolate Coffee Cake

Cake

⅔ cup packed brown sugar

10 egg yolks

1 vanilla bean, opened, seeds
    scraped out and reserved

¾ cup flour

3 egg whites

6 ounces chocolate chips
    (about 1 cup)

Cream Filling

8 tablespoons (1 stick) butter

1 cup confectioners' sugar, plus
    extra for dusting the cake

2 tablespoons instant coffee

2 tablespoons unsweetened
    dark cocoa powder

Please, for extra happiness have a slice of this with a glass of cold milk.

Preheat the oven to 350°F.

MAKE THE CAKE: Beat the brown sugar with 6 of the egg yolks and the vanilla seeds until the mixture is very creamy and fluffy. Not all of the sugar will be dissolved, which is okay.

Add the flour to the yolk and sugar mixture and mix to combine. In a separate bowl, whip the egg whites to stiff peaks, then fold them carefully into the batter.

Butter an 8-inch springform pan, then turn the batter into the pan. Pour the chocolate chips on top, spreading them evenly, and bake for 20 to 25 minutes. Remove the sides of the pan to let the cake cool.

MAKE THE CREAM FILLING: Beat the butter with a handheld or stand mixer. Whisk in the remaining 4 egg yolks until they are foamy, then add the confectioners' sugar. When the mixture is smooth, stir in the coffee and cocoa powder.

Slice the cake into three layers. Spread each with the coffee cream and reassemble the cake. Press lightly as you put each layer back, so that the layers will stick together. Dust the cake with confectioners' sugar before serving.

Sticky Buns

MAKES APPROXIMATELY
8 ROLLS

A little bit of a hangover after a great night and lots of wine also requires something sweet in the morning without too much work. These are ready in a little over 30 minutes, really no time at all. And usually everything will be in the pantry, so you don't have to leave the house, either—an ideal breakfast!

If you're really thinking ahead, you can make the dough the night before so they'll be ready to be popped in the oven from the fridge in the morning.

MAKE THE BUNS: Preheat the oven to 350°F. In a food processor or by hand, mix the flour with a pinch of salt, the baking powder, and the chilled butter until the dough looks like coarse sand. Slowly add the buttermilk, stopping when the dough is springy but not wet.

On a countertop dusted with flour, roll the dough ball out into a ¼-inch-thick slab.

Spread the cream cheese on the dough then sprinkle with the brown sugar, cinnamon, and chopped nuts.

Roll up the dough lengthwise into a long cylinder.

Butter a baking sheet or cover with parchment paper. Cut the roll into equal slices and place them flat on the baking sheet, so the swirl in each one is facing up (like a Cinnabon, only better!). Brush with the lightly beaten egg and bake the rolls for about 25 to 30 minutes until golden brown and cooked on the inside. Remove them from the oven and let them cool while you make the glaze.

MAKE THE GLAZE: In a saucepan melt the brown sugar with the butter and cream. Pour the glaze on the buns once they have cooled.

Buns
2½ cups flour

Pinch of kosher salt

3 teaspoons baking powder

6 tablespoons butter, chilled and cut into cubes

⅔ to ¾ cup buttermilk

½ cup cream cheese, at room temperature

¼ cup packed brown sugar

1 teaspoon ground cinnamon

½ cup nuts (walnuts, pecans, whatever you have), coarsely chopped

1 whole egg plus 2 yolks, lightly beaten

Glaze
⅔ cup packed brown sugar

3 tablespoons butter

2 tablespoons heavy cream

Savory Mini Muffins

3 tablespoons grated Parmesan
    cheese

¼ cup plus 3 tablespoons flour

1 teaspoon baking soda

3 tablespoons butter, softened

2 egg yolks

¾ cup milk

6 sun-dried tomatoes (page
    13) finely chopped (if you
    use store-bought sun-dried
    tomatoes packed in oil,
    squeeze out as much oil as
    you can)

2 tablespoons finely chopped
    fresh chives

1 teaspoon garlic powder

1 teaspoon onion powder

Kosher salt and freshly ground
    black pepper

These little muffins will come out very soft, almost like little soufflés. I had these in a restaurant in New Orleans and I came back to California with a craving for them. Thanks to the expertise of the best pastry chef I ever had, Bambi Hosaka, I can now serve these to everybody in America. Thank you, Bambi!

Preheat the oven to 325°F.

Reserve 2 tablespoons of the grated Parmesan.

Place the remaining tablespoon of Parmesan, flour, baking soda, butter, egg yolks, milk, tomatoes, chives, garlic powder, onion powder, and salt and pepper to taste in a blender and whip into a nice batter, making sure there are no lumps. Using a spoon, fill each cup of a nonstick mini muffin pan two-thirds full with the batter.

Bake until golden brown, 8 to 10 minutes.

Sprinkle with the reserved Parmesan while hot and serve.

Fig, Strawberry, and Honey Butter

This is good for almost everything that goes well with a sweet flavor, but my favorite way to use it is in the morning on a piece of crusty bread.

Place the figs in a heatproof bowl and pour a cup of boiling water over them. Let them sit for 5 minutes, then drain them and squeeze out the excess water.

Combine the figs and strawberries in a bowl with the honey, cinnamon, and nutmeg, a pinch of salt, and the butter. Transfer the mixture to a sheet of plastic wrap, roll it into a log, and enclose in the wrap. Leave to cool in the refrigerator and cut into slices before using.

1½ cups dried figs, finely chopped
½ cup chopped strawberries
1 tablespoon honey
1 teaspoon ground cinnamon
½ teaspoon freshly grated nutmeg
Kosher salt
8 tablespoons (1 stick) butter, softened

SWEET ENDINGS

Dessert

I USE THE SAME WORD TO DESCRIBE MY GRANDMA AND DESSERTS—
sweet. Both are always there for you, have the capacity to comfort you any time, and take all your troubles away in a matter of minutes. It's hard for me to think of a sweet I don't like! Most chefs choose one concentration over the other—either savory foods or pastries. Not me—I like doing it all.

For me, dessert can be summed up in four words: sweet, tangy, crunchy, creamy. Almost any dessert I make or enjoy has at least two of these words associated with it, and together, they equal 100 percent satisfaction. Dessert can be simple, like fruit paired with citrus and a sugar crumble. Or it can be rich, like a dense piece of pound cake that will make your mouth water and have you dreaming of clouds of chocolate raining tiny droplets of lemon curd.

What I'm saying is that there is tons of variety when it comes to dessert; cakes, cookies, biscuits, ice creams, and so many more that I can't keep up. America likes to make things very, very sweet while in Italy, we like to partner the slightly savory with a touch of sweet by using things like toasted hazelnuts and pine nuts or serving a sweet dish like vanilla panna cotta with balsamic syrup. That's my kind of way to end a meal. Speaking of endings, dessert is your last chance in a meal for the wow factor. It's the last bite everyone takes of the meal and will leave that lasting impression on your guests. You gotta make sure it's spot-on.

For a sure home run, chocolate is arguably the king (or queen!) of the dessert world. It melts, crunches, coats, and shaves like gold. (Plus, it doubles as an "I'm sorry for forgetting our anniversary" escape plan. You won't be out of the dog house, but at least you will earn yourself a little wiggle room.) There's dark chocolate, milk chocolate, semisweet chocolate, and all of the above mixed with whatever other ingredients you can think of that can be used in pastries. I'm not suggesting covering your green beans with it, but if you find yourself in a dessert bind, with no time to make one of these recipes, shave chocolate over fruit, dust it with confectioners' sugar, and you're good to go.

Most of all, dessert is about love. At my dinner table, it's all about family. Your family isn't worried about what altitude your strawberries grew at or what speed you whipped the cream at. They just want to be happy in your company and dessert is the perfect way to make that happen. Take those sweets, those crunchy bits, those pieces of brûléed sugar and use them to make their faces light up. It's very basic, guys: like my grandpa told me: "Fabio, keep it simple. Love will be the greatest ingredient you will ever cook with." Grandpa, you couldn't have been more right, and all of my desserts will always have that most important ingredient, even if you don't see it listed in the recipe.

Boston Vanilla Cream Pie

**SERVES 8;
OR FABIO ALONE ON
A SUNDAY MORNING**

To grate the chocolate for this recipe, get a big chunk and do it with a regular cheese grater. Boom!

Preheat the oven to 350°F. Butter and flour a 9- or 10-inch spring-form cake pan.

In a bowl, beat the eggs, sugar, and salt with an electric mixer (or a really fast grandma) until fluffy and pale in color, 5 to 7 minutes.

Heat the milk and the vanilla seeds in a pot over medium-low heat and whisk to help the vanilla infuse the milk. Be careful not to boil it. When it is warm, pour it slowly into the egg mixture while continuing to beat with the electric mixer. Gently fold in the sifted flour.

Pour the batter into the prepared pan and bake for 20 to 25 minutes, or until the center feels firm to the touch. Transfer the pan to a wire rack to cool for 20 minutes. Run a serrated knife around the edge to loosen the cake. Once it is out of the pan, cut it into 3 layers and let them cool completely.

Place one layer on a plate and spread with one-third of the crème anglaise. Top with another layer, another third of the crème anglaise, then the third layer and the remaining crème anglaise. Chill the cake until the crème anglaise is set, about 30 minutes. Remove the cake from the refrigerator.

If you want to add grated chocolate you're going to purgatory for piggishness but it is totally worth it.

Butter, for greasing the pan
4 eggs
1 cup packed brown sugar
½ teaspoon kosher salt
¼ cup plus 2 tablespoons milk
2 vanilla beans, split lengthwise, seeds scraped and
   reserved
1 cup flour, sifted, plus more
   for dusting
1 recipe Fabio's Quick Crème
   Anglaise (page 241)
Grated semisweet chocolate,
   for garnish (optional)

Maple Bundt Cake

1½ cups cake flour, plus 2
  tablespoons for dusting
2 teaspoons baking powder
1 teaspoon baking soda
1 teaspoon kosher salt
12 tablespoons (1½ sticks)
  butter, softened, plus more
  for the pan
⅔ cup packed brown sugar
3 large eggs
⅔ cup pure maple syrup
2 teaspoons pure vanilla
  extract
1 cup sour cream
½ cup cold heavy cream

When most people use a Bundt cake pan, when the cake is done, they serve it so the bigger hole is on top. I like to serve it so the smaller hole is on top and the glaze stays in the middle of the cake as well. That way I also have more surface area on the top to hold the glaze so not as much runs off the cake.

Preheat the oven to 350°F. Butter and flour a 10-inch Bundt cake pan.

In a medium bowl, whisk together the flour, baking powder, baking soda, and salt.

In a stand mixer fitted with the paddle beat the butter and brown sugar on medium-high speed until fluffy, about 5 minutes. Add the eggs, one at a time, again beating until fluffy.

Beat in ⅓ cup of the maple syrup and the vanilla. Add the flour mixture in two parts, then the sour cream.

Pour the batter into the mold and bake until golden brown, 30 to 35 minutes. Remove the cake from the oven and let it rest and cool for 20 minutes before removing it from the pan.

Just before serving, whip the cold cream until fluffy; add the remaining ⅓ cup maple syrup, and beat until it is all incorporated.

Now go paint the cake with it and enjoy!

Pound Cake

When I first saw this recipe, I thought we needed to use one pound of every ingredient and the result was a disaster. Now we got it all figured out! For a garnish, try smashing some berries with a fork and mixing them into whipped cream.

---

1 pound (4 sticks) butter, softened, plus more for the pans

2½ cups sugar

2 teaspoons pure vanilla extract

10 eggs, at room temperature, lightly beaten

3½ cups flour

1 tablespoon kosher salt

Preheat the oven to 325°F. Butter two 9 × 5-inch loaf pans.

In the bowl of a stand mixer, fitted with the paddle, whip together the butter and sugar on medium-high speed until light and fluffy. Turn the mixer speed to medium, add the vanilla, and beat to combine.

Add the eggs in three batches, mixing well between each one. Reduce the speed to low and add the flour in four additions, mixing just until incorporated. Add the salt and mix once more to combine.

Divide the batter evenly between the two prepared loaf pans. It will be very thick so a spoon works best.

Bake the loaves for 1 hour, or until a toothpick inserted in the center of each cake comes out clean.

Carrot Cake with Pecans and Cream Cheese Frosting

2½ cups flour, plus more for dusting

2 teaspoons baking powder

1 teaspoon baking soda

1½ teaspoons ground cinnamon

1 teaspoon kosher salt

½ teaspoon freshly grated nutmeg

¾ pound (3 sticks) butter, at room temperature, plus more for the pan

½ cup granulated sugar

1½ cups packed brown sugar

3 whole eggs plus 2 egg yolks

2 teaspoons pure vanilla extract

3 cups grated carrots

½ cup water

1 cup finely chopped pecans

Fabio's Cream Cheese Frosting (recipe follows)

Very simple and very delicious, this carrot cake is loaded with tons of carrots and the sweet taste of pecans.

Preheat the oven to 350°F. Butter and flour an 8- or 9-inch springform pan.

Whisk together the flour, baking powder, baking soda, cinnamon, salt, and nutmeg in a medium bowl.

In the bowl of a stand mixer fitted with the paddle, cream the butter, granulated sugar, and brown sugar on medium speed until they are fluffy and the sugar has almost dissolved. Add the eggs and egg yolks while continuing to beat, mixing until the eggs are absorbed.

Add the vanilla, carrots, and water and beat until well combined, about 3 minutes. Reduce the speed to low and add the flour mixture, then the pecans, beating just until combined. Pour the batter into the prepared pan.

Bake until the top of the cake is golden brown and a toothpick inserted into the center comes out clean, about 30 minutes. When it is done baking, turn off the oven and allow the cake to cool down for another 15 minutes in the turned off oven with the door open.

With a serrated knife remove the cake from the pan (maybe the bottom is a bit sticky; just run the knife under it).

Using a long serrated knife, cut the cake in half to create two layers. Frost the bottom layer with half of the frosting, then place the top layer on it and frost the top of the cake with the remaining frosting.

— {Continued} —

Cream Cheese Frosting

In a stand mixer, beat the butter, cream cheese, and mascarpone together until light and fluffy. Turn down the speed to low, and incorporate the confectioners' sugar and vanilla.

8 tablespoons (1 stick) butter, softened

8 ounces cream cheese, softened

2 ounces mascarpone cheese, softened

2½ cups confectioners' sugar, sifted

2 teaspoons pure vanilla extract

Date and Lemon Ricotta Cake

Cake

1 tablespoon softened butter

1 tablespoon melted butter

1 cup packed light or dark brown sugar

4½ cups ricotta cheese

1½ cups refrigerated Lemon Curd (page 231)

2 teaspoons pure vanilla extract

Finely grated zest of 1 lemon

⅓ cup cornstarch

6 whole eggs plus 2 egg yolks

Topping

3 cups pitted dates

2 teaspoons Grand Marnier or Marsala

1 cup packed light brown sugar

2 cinnamon sticks

¾ cup water

3 teaspoons gelatin powder

T his has got to be one of my ultimate favorites. I'm into creamy desserts like cheesecake and Boston Cream Pie, but the reality is that they're heavy. A ricotta cake is the best of both worlds. It's very thick and creamy, but super light. You can eat a pound of it and not even feel it. It's a perfect dessert to finish a very nice, rich meal. You can also chop the dates if you prefer, which spreads them more evenly over the cake.

MAKE THE CAKE: Preheat the oven to 325°F. Butter a 9-inch springform pan. Cut a sheet of parchment paper to fit the pan, place in the bottom and butter again using the melted butter and a pastry brush.

Combine the brown sugar, ricotta, lemon curd, vanilla, lemon zest, cornstarch, eggs, and egg yolks into a smooth batter. Pour into the pan.

Bake for 45 minutes to 1 hour, or until the cake is fully set. (A good way to check for this is to shake the pan a little bit. If the cake doesn't wiggle in the middle, it's done.)

Let the cake cool in the pan for 15 minutes, then carefully remove the sides of the pan. Transfer the cake to a plate to cool completely.

MAKE THE TOPPING: Mix the dates with the Grand Marnier or Marsala and set aside.

In a saucepan bring the light brown sugar and cinnamon sticks to a boil with the water, then reduce until almost all the liquid has evaporated and the mixture looks like caramel sauce. Add the dates and the Grand Marnier or Marsala and allow the mixture to thicken slightly. Dissolve the gelatin in 2 to 3 tablespoons of warm water and add to the saucepan.

— {Continued} —

Remove the cinnamon sticks and discard. Arrange the dates on the cake. Coat the cake with the gelatin mixture and allow to set before slicing the cake.

Lemon Curd

MAKES 1½ CUPS CURD

6 egg yolks

1 cup sugar

1 tablespoon finely grated lemon zest

1 teaspoon pure vanilla extract

Juice of 3 large lemons (⅓ to ½ cup), strained of seeds and pulp

4 tablespoons (½ stick) butter, cut into cubes

Pinch of kosher salt

Whisk together the egg yolks, sugar, lemon zest, vanilla, and lemon juice in a heat resistant bowl.

Fill a saucepan large enough to hold the bowl about one-quarter full with water. Place on high heat and bring the water to a boil, then reduce it to a very low simmer. Place the bowl on the saucepan over the simmering water and cook, stirring with a wooden spoon, until the mixture thickens enough to coat the back of the spoon, no more than 8 to 10 minutes.

Once the mixture has thickened, remove it from heat and add the butter 2 cubes at a time, stirring to incorporate. Add a pinch of salt, stir, and allow the curd to cool completely.

Roasted Banana Rum Cake

MAKES 1 LOAF

love eating this along with some jasmine tea. It's very good even after a few days, when it has started to dry out—just spread it with a touch of melted butter.

Preheat the oven to 375°F.

Toss the bananas with the 2 tablespoons of granulated sugar, then spread them on a baking pan and roast for 25 to 30 minutes until they are browned and the sugar has caramelized a little. Remove and set aside.

Cover the bottom of a 9 × 5-inch loaf pan with parchment paper, then butter and flour it.

In a small saucepan over low heat, heat the raisins, rum, and brown sugar. Once the mixture has boiled, remove it from the heat and let the raisins steep for at least 1 hour.

In a stand mixer fitted with the paddle, combine the bananas, raisins, pecans, flour, baking powder, salt, butter, the remaining 1 cup granulated sugar, vanilla, eggs, egg yolks, lemon zest, juice, and cream on medium-low speed. Pour the batter into the prepared pan and bake for an hour. The cake is done when a skewer poked into it comes up clean. If it does not, continue baking, checking for doneness every 5 minutes.

Let the cake cool for 5 minutes after it comes out of the oven, then transfer the pan to a rack and let the cake cool completely. Remove the cake from the pan.

4 ripe bananas, peeled and chopped

1 cup plus 2 tablespoons granulated sugar

½ cup raisins

⅓ cup rum

¼ cup packed brown sugar

1 cup chopped pecans

1⅛ cups flour plus extra for dusting the pan

2 teaspoons baking powder

½ teaspoon kosher salt

8 tablespoons (1 stick) butter, melted

1 tablespoon pure vanilla extract

2 whole eggs plus 2 egg yolks

Finely grated zest and juice of 1 lemon

½ cup heavy cream

Strawberry Shortcake

Berries

3 cups fresh strawberries, hulled and quartered

⅓ cup fresh lemon juice

⅓ cup sugar

Biscuits

2 cups flour plus more for dusting

¼ cup plus 2 tablespoons sugar

2 tablespoons baking powder

½ teaspoon kosher salt

7 tablespoons (1 stick less 1 tablespoon) cold butter, cut into small pieces

1 cup plus 2 tablespoons heavy cream

1 whole egg plus 2 egg yolks

To serve

½ cup cold heavy cream

I've made this recipe in thirty minutes flat. If you can let the berries macerate overnight, it's better, but if you have no time, crush a few of them with a fork and some lemon juice, then toss the rest in with the sugar.

PREPARE THE BERRIES: Toss the quartered strawberries in a large bowl with the lemon juice and sugar to combine. Let macerate at room temperature for about 2 hours.

PREPARE THE BISCUITS: Preheat the oven to 375°F. Line a baking sheet with parchment paper.

Whisk together the flour, sugar, baking powder, and salt in a medium bowl. In a food processor fitted with the blade attachment, cut the butter into the flour mixture until it resembles coarse meal. Transfer to a bowl, add 1 cup of the cream, and, using a wooden spoon, combine just until the dough starts to come together but is still crumbly.

Turn out the dough onto a lightly floured surface and pat into a rough 6-inch square, about 1 inch thick. Cut 4 biscuits from dough and place them on the lined baking sheet. (You can reshape the dough pieces left over and make another biscuit or two.) Whisk together the egg and egg yolks and remaining 2 tablespoons cream, then brush egg wash over tops of dough rounds.

Bake until the tops of the biscuits are golden brown, about 25 minutes, rotating the sheet pan halfway through the baking time. Transfer the biscuits to a wire rack and let cool slightly.

When ready to serve, whip the cold cream in a chilled bowl until medium peaks form. Split biscuits in half and place a bottom half on each plate. Cover with berries and drizzle them with juice, then top with the biscuit tops and dollops of whipped cream. Scatter a few more strawberries on top and more juice if you like.

Pear-Hazelnut Tart

SERVES 6

The half pears in this tart make a dramatic, beautiful presentation. They also work well to mark off portion sizes—a slice with one half for each person. For added sweetness you can dust the tart with confectioners' sugar, or, if you want to take it to the next level, drizzle it with some melted chocolate.

Preheat the oven to 350°F. Butter a 9-inch tart pan with a removable bottom.

MAKE THE PASTRY: In a food processor or stand mixer fitted with the paddle attachment, combine the flour, sugar, butter, egg, and salt until they come together to make a ball. Remove the dough and set aside.

MAKE THE PEARS: Combine the wine, sugar, cinnamon stick, and mint in a pot large enough to hold all the pears and bring to a boil. Place the pears into the pot, lower the heat to medium, and poach for 30 minutes. Remove the pears and set aside until they are cool enough to handle. Then cut each one in half, remove the seeds and core, and set aside.

MAKE THE FILLING: In a food processor, grind the hazelnuts and brown sugar into a smooth, fine powder and transfer to a bowl. Add the vanilla, flour, butter, eggs, egg yolks, ricotta, and pine nuts and stir until well combined.

On a floured countertop, roll the dough out into a 12-inch circle.

Gently fit the dough into the tart pan, and tuck in any overhang. Spoon the filling into the dough-lined pan and smooth the top. Lay the pear halves on top of the filling, close together, stem ends toward the center. Bake the tart until it is golden brown, about 35 minutes. Allow the tart to cool completely on a rack before serving.

Pastry
1⅓ cups flour
½ cup sugar
8 tablespoons (1 stick) butter
1 egg
Pinch of kosher salt

Pears
6 cups red wine
½ cup sugar
1 cinnamon stick
20 fresh mint leaves
4 firm Bosc or Williams pears, peeled

Filling
1 cup hazelnuts
⅓ cup packed brown sugar
2 teaspoons pure vanilla extract
⅓ cup plus 1 tablespoon flour
8 tablespoons (1 stick) butter, at room temperature
2 whole eggs plus 2 egg yolks
½ cup ricotta cheese
½ cup pine nuts

Espresso Coffee Granita

MAKES ABOUT 1 QUART; SERVES 8

1 cup simple syrup
3 cups very strong hot espresso coffee

To make simple syrup, just combine equal parts water and sugar, bring it to a boil, let it cool down, and voila!

Stir the syrup into the coffee then set it aside to cool. Pour the cooled coffee into a pan or a wide shallow container that will fit on a shelf in the freezer. Slide the pan into the freezer.

The liquid will become slushy around the edges within 2 hours or so. Scrape the granita with a fork where it is beginning to freeze. Continue stirring, scraping and breaking up any lumps every 20 to 25 minutes, until the granita has frozen icy crystals throughout. The whole process will take 3 to 4 hours, depending on how many times you open the freezer to peek—naughty! Serve in chilled glasses with gelato on top if you want.

Vanilla Fritters with Prosecco Cream

Louisiana and apple fritters have nothing on these. They are addictive.

Preheat the oil in a deep sauté pan to 375°F. Line a sheet pan with paper towels or set a wire rack over a sheet pan.

Melt the butter with the milk in a saucepan over low heat. Add the sugar, vanilla, lemon zest, and salt. Remove the pan from the heat and stir in the flour with a whisk, making sure there are no lumps.

Using a hand mixer or a lot of elbow grease, beat in the egg yolks one by one.

Beat the egg whites in a separate bowl until stiff and carefully spoon the foam into the batter. Stir to combine, then use the mixer again to fully combine the ingredients.

Using an ice cream scoop spoon small balls of dough into the hot oil.

Fry the fritters for a few minutes turning them often until golden brown and cooked. Transfer them to the paper towel–lined baking sheet or rack to cool, then dust with confectioners' sugar. Serve with Fabio's Prosecco cream.

2 cups light olive oil, for frying
4 tablespoons (½ stick) butter
1 cup milk
2 tablespoons sugar
4 teaspoons pure vanilla extract
Finely grated zest of 1 lemon
Pinch of kosher salt
1⅔ cups flour
4 eggs, separated
½ cup confectioners' sugar
½ recipe Fabio's Prosecco Cream (recipe follows)

Fabio's Prosecco Cream

In a heavy saucepan, beat the eggs and sugar with a portable mixer until thick. Gradually beat in the Prosecco. Place the saucepan over low heat. Beat on low speed with the mixer for 2 minutes. Continue beating over low heat until the mixture reaches 160°F, about 6 minutes.

Cool instantly by putting the pan into a larger bowl filled with ice water. Add the orange zest, and stir in the whipped cream and continue to cool. Cover with plastic wrap and store in the refrigerator until ready to use.

10 egg yolks
½ cup sugar
1 cup Prosecco
Finely grated zest of 1 orange
1 cup heavy cream, whipped

Quick Crème Anglaise

2 cups milk

2 vanilla beans, seeds scraped
out and reserved

7 egg yolks

⅓ cup sugar

1 tablespoon Grand Marnier

Like risotto, if you can stir, you can make this. If you can't stir you don't deserve sweets. This is delicious spooned over berries, pound cake, or chocolate cake. Or, if you want to let it set in the fridge overnight, you can use it as a pudding.

In a saucepan over medium heat, bring the milk, vanilla seeds, and bean pods to a simmer.

In a medium heatproof bowl, combine the egg yolks and sugar and beat until foamy. While continuing to beat, gradually add the hot vanilla milk in a thin stream.

Pour the mixture back into the saucepan and place over low heat. Stir slowly and constantly, until the mixture thickens, 5 to 8 minutes. Remove the pan from the heat and allow to cool for at least an hour. The sauce will thicken slightly. Add the Grand Marnier and stir to combine.

To store, place a sheet of plastic wrap directly on the surface of the mixture to prevent a skin from forming. The crème anglaise will keep in the refrigerator for 3 to 4 days.

Variation:

FOR COFFEE CRÈME ANGLAISE: Follow the same recipe, but when you return the mixture to low heat, add ½ cup espresso beans. Remove these from the sauce before using or storing.

Italian Chocolate and Caramel Pudding

SERVES 6

It seems like a crazy idea, but when you take your first bite of this pudding you really taste the balsamic and then you have the sweet finish. I suggest you make more of the caramel than you need. Then you can keep it in the fridge in a squeeze bottle and just heat it up in the microwave whenever you need it. Because who doesn't like more caramel?

Softened butter, for the ramekins
2½ cups milk
Zest of 1 blood orange (a regular orange is okay, too)
1 teaspoon pure vanilla extract
2 teaspoons balsamic vinegar
½ cup superfine sugar
1 cup Fabio's Caramel Sauce, plus the rest for drizzling (page 244)
½ cup fresh orange juice
3 whole eggs plus 2 egg yolks
½ cup chocolate chips

Lightly butter 6 ramekins.

Put the milk into a saucepan with the orange zest, vanilla, and vinegar. Bring to a boil, then remove from heat and stir in ¼ cup of the sugar; set aside for at least 40 minutes to infuse.

Combine the caramel sauce with the orange juice and divide evenly among the ramekins, swirling to cover the bottom of each one.

Return the pan of infused milk to low heat, and bring to a simmer. Beat the whole eggs and egg yolks together and pour the warm milk into the eggs, whisking constantly. Strain into a bowl and set aside.

Preheat the oven to 325°F. Place 10 to 12 chocolate chips on the bottom of each ramekin, then fill each one to the top with pudding mixture.

Place the ramekins in a roasting pan and pour in boiling water to come halfway up the sides of the ramekins. Bake the puddings for about 1 hour, or until they have set. Remove, cool, then place in the fridge to chill overnight.

Before serving drizzle the top with more caramel sauce.

— {Continued} —

Fabio's Caramel Sauce

In a medium saucepan, combine the butter and sugar. Begin to melt the mixture over medium heat, slowly bringing the mixture to a boil. Once boiling, continue cooking at this heat, stirring constantly, for about 3 minutes.

Slowly drizzle in the cream. Continue cooking until the mixture has slightly thickened. Remove the sauce from the heat and transfer to a bowl or other container for cooling. Stir in the allspice and vanilla while it cools. The sauce will keep in the refrigerator for up to 2 months.

8 tablespoons (1 stick) butter, cut into medium-size cubes

2½ cups sugar

1 cup heavy cream, at room temperature

1 teaspoon ground allspice

1 teaspoon pure vanilla extract

Best Key Lime Pie

Crust

2 cups graham cracker crumbs

2 tablespoons sugar

7 tablespoons (1 stick less 1
   tablespoon) butter, melted

Filling

5 egg yolks

¼ cup sugar

2 cups sweetened condensed
   milk

⅓ cup fresh key lime juice

1 cup heavy cream, chilled

I normally don't like key lime, but this recipe has a perfect balance
between the sour citrus flavor and the sweetness.

Preheat the oven to 350°F.

MAKE THE CRUST: Stir together the graham cracker crumbs, sugar,
and butter in a bowl with a fork until combined well, then press
mixture evenly onto bottom and up the sides of a 9-inch round cake
pan.

MAKE THE FILLING: Whisk together the egg yolks and sugar until
they start to foam and increase in volume. Add the condensed milk
and mix until well combined. Add the lime juice and whisk again
to combine.

Pour the filling into the crust and bake the pie for 15 minutes.
Remove from the oven and cool the pie completely on a rack; the
filling will set as it cools.

Cover the pan with plastic wrap and then chill in the refrigerator for at least 4 hours. Just before serving, beat the heavy cream in
a bowl with an electric mixer just until it holds stiff peaks. Serve the
pie topped with cream.

Really Easy Mississippi Mud Pie

I love chocolate so this probably will be my wedding dessert. Serve this warm with a scoop of ice cream or whipped cream flavored with a touch of sweet liquor like Grand Marnier or Kahlua.

Preheat the oven to 350°F.

MAKE THE CRUST: Combine the crushed Oreos and melted butter, then cover the bottom of a 9-inch springform pan with the mixture, pressing the crumb mixture down a bit.

MAKE THE FILLING: In a saucepan over low heat, melt the butter and chocolate, stirring often, until well blended.

In a bowl, beat the eggs and yolks until they are frothy. Stir in the honey or agave, brown sugar, and vanilla. Add the chocolate mixture to the egg and sugar mixture, and stir to combine well.

Pour the filling into the crust and bake for 35 to 40 minutes, or until the top is slightly crunchy and the filling is set.

Serve warm with a scoop of ice cream or dollop of whipped cream.

Crust
30 Oreo cookies, including filling, crushed
½ cup melted butter

Filling
6 tablespoons (¾ stick) butter
3 ounces unsweetened chocolate
3 whole eggs plus 2 egg yolks
3 tablespoons agave nectar or light honey
1⅓ cups packed brown sugar
1 teaspoon pure vanilla extract

Brûléed Peach Pie

Crust

2⅔ cups flour

3 teaspoons plus 1 tablespoon sugar

1 teaspoon kosher salt

8 tablespoons (1 stick) cold butter, cut into ½-inch pieces

3 ounces extra-virgin olive oil

½ cup really *really* cold water

Filling

6 large, ripe peaches or 8 medium, peeled, pitted, and sliced into eighths

1 cup plus 1 tablespoon granulated sugar

4 teaspoons fresh lemon juice

½ cup flour

2 tablespoons butter, sliced into slivers

1 egg yolk, beaten with 1 tablespoon water

This is what apple pie in America wants to be when it dies and goes to heaven. The Italian dough is sweeter than American dough, and when you "brûlée" something, it means it's been cooking in sugar. Italian dough, sugar, and peaches. Do I need to say anything more?

MAKE THE CRUST: In a food processor, pulse the flour with the sugar and salt until combined. Add the butter and oil and pulse until the mixture resembles coarse meal. Transfer the mixture to a large bowl and sprinkle the ice water on top. Stir with a fork until a crumbly dough forms.

Turn the dough out onto a work surface and press it into a ball. Cut the dough in half and form it into 2 disks. Wrap the disks in plastic wrap and refrigerate 30 minutes.

Roll out one section of the dough to a circle about 12 inches in diameter and line a 9-inch pie pan. Place the pan in the refrigerator to chill the dough.

Preheat the oven to 350°F.

MAKE THE FILLING: Place the peaches in a large bowl. Add 1 cup of the sugar, lemon juice, and flour, toss well, and let stand for 5 minutes.

Pour the peaches and their juices into the chilled pie shell and scatter the butter slices on top. Brush the edge of the pie shell with some of the egg yolk mixture. Roll out the second disk of pie dough and place it over the filling.

— {Continued} —

Press the edges of the dough together to seal. Don't worry if there is a bit of overhang—leave it to become brown and delicious in the oven! Brush the remaining egg wash on the top crust and cut diagonal scores to help vent the steam out as it bakes. Sprinkle with 1 tablespoon of sugar.

Bake the pie for about 25 minutes, then cover with aluminum foil to prevent the sugar from burning and bake another 20 minutes.

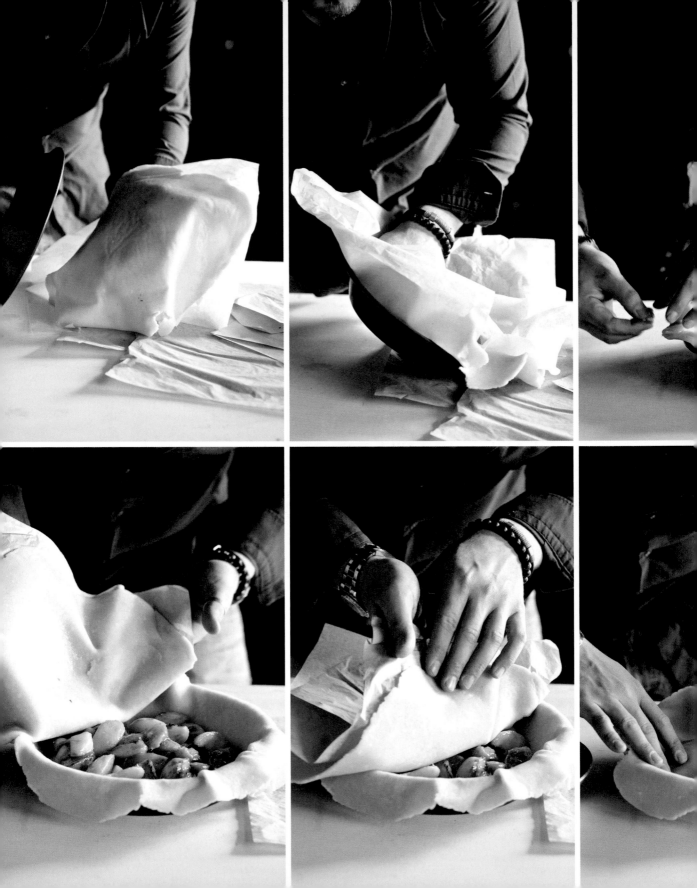

Cheddar Cheese Apple Pie with a Hint of Parmesan

Apple pie gets a makeover! This can be served during the meal as a sweeter side, especially for the holidays.

Preheat the oven to 450°F.

On a lightly floured work surface, work the dough in 2 separate balls and roll until wide enough to be able to cut a circle from each round about 12 inches in diameter.

Place one round in the bottom of a 9- or 10-inch springform pan; the edges will come up the sides and that's OK. Refrigerate the dough-lined pan, and the other dough circle for at least 15 minutes.

Peel and core the apples and cut them into ¼-inch-thick slices. Toss them with the lime juice.

In a separate bowl combine the brown sugar, flour, and nutmeg. Add the mixture to the apples and mix well, making sure that all the dry ingredients are absorbed by the lime juice. Let rest for 15 minutes.

Put the apple filling into the cake pan and flatten it with your hand a bit. Sprinkle the butter, cheddar cheese, and Parmesan on top of the apples and top with the other circle of dough, tucking it in to form a kind of dough package around the apples.

Using a paring knife, cut several steam vents in top of dough. Lightly brush surface with egg wash.

Bake the pie for about 15 to 20 minutes until the top crust starts to get lightly browned.

Reduce the oven to 350°F, rotate the pie, and continue baking until the crust is golden brown and the juices are bubbling, about 1¼ hours.

Transfer to a wire rack to cool completely before serving, sprinkled with more Parmesan if desired.

1 recipe Fabio's Savory Pie Dough (recipe follows)

15 medium green sour apples

Juice of 3 limes

¼ cup superfine brown sugar (regular brown sugar is fine if you can't find it)

⅓ cup flour

1 teaspoon freshly grated nutmeg

4 tablespoons (½ stick) cold butter, cut into small pieces

1 cup grated sharp cheddar cheese

2 tablespoons grated Parmesan cheese

2 egg yolks, beaten with 3 tablespoons water

Savory Pie Dough

2 cups flour

½ teaspoon fine salt

¼ teaspoon freshly grated
   nutmeg

8 tablespoons (1 stick) butter,
   cut into tiny cubes

¼ cup ice water

Combine the flour, salt, nutmeg, and butter in a food processor and pulse together until the mixture has the consistency of wet sand. Drizzle in the water until a ball of dough forms.

Take out the dough, pressing any loose bits onto the ball. Wrap in plastic and refrigerate until ready to use.

Chocolate Currant Cookies

1½ cups packed brown sugar

12 tablespoons (1½ sticks)
    butter

2 whole eggs plus 2 egg yolks

1 tablespoon honey

1 teaspoon pure vanilla extract

2 cups flour

⅔ cup dried currants

1 cup unsweetened cocoa
    powder

½ teaspoon kosher salt

1 teaspoon baking powder

2 tablespoons confectioners'
    sugar

Keep these in a jar in the kitchen and grab one every time you pass by.

In a bowl, beat together the brown sugar and butter until fluffy. Add the eggs, egg yolks, honey, and vanilla and beat to combine.

In a separate bowl, whisk together the flour, currants, cocoa powder, salt, and baking powder. Stir the dry mixture into the butter mixture gradually, then mix to combine thoroughly.

Cover the bowl with plastic wrap and place the dough in the refrigerator to chill for 30 minutes.

Preheat the oven to 350°F. Line a baking sheet with parchment paper or a Silpat.

Roll the chilled dough into 12 equal balls, then place the balls several inches apart on the prepared baking sheet. Bake for 7 to 10 minutes. Transfer the cookies to a wire rack to cool, then dust them with the confectioners' sugar just before serving.

Italian Wedding Cookies

12 tablespoons (1½ sticks)
   butter
½ cup light olive oil
⅔ cup granulated sugar
⅓ cup confectioners' sugar
4 egg yolks
1 teaspoon pure vanilla extract
2 teaspoons finely grated
   lemon zest
3 cups cake flour
2 teaspoons baking powder
½ teaspoon sea salt
Drizzle of extra-virgin olive oil

We aren't serving them at my wedding, but they are delicious and easy to make so you might want to think about it if you're planning one yourself.

In a bowl, beat together the butter, light olive oil, granulated sugar, and confectioners' sugar until fluffy. Add the egg yolks, vanilla, and lemon zest and beat to combine.

In a separate bowl, whisk together the cake flour, baking powder, and salt. Stir into the butter and egg mixture until well combined. Cover the dough with plastic wrap and refrigerate for 30 minutes.

Preheat oven to 325°F. Line a baking sheet with parchment paper or a Silpat mat. Form 12 balls out of the dough, then flatten each one and make an indentation with your thumb in the middle. Sprinkle each cookie with sea salt, then place them several inches apart on the prepared baking sheet and bake for 20 to 25 minutes. Let the cookies cool and then drizzle with extra-virgin olive oil just before serving.

Grandma's Sugar Sprinkled Cookies

This is just as simple as it gets. Eggs, flour, sugar and bake. We had no means to get treats when I was a kid, so we had these because fresh eggs were in the backyard, we always had sugar even when we were broke, and my mom would make butter by whipping milk.

In the bowl of a stand mixer fitted with the paddle, beat together the butter and brown sugar until fluffy. Add the lemon zest, vanilla, and 5 of the egg yolks and continue beating at medium speed until well combined.

In a separate bowl, whisk together the flour, baking powder, and salt. Stir into the butter and egg mixture gradually. Cover the bowl with plastic wrap and place the dough in the refrigerator for 30 minutes.

Preheat the oven to 350°F. Form 12 balls and flatten them with the palm of your hand. Beat together the egg and the remaining egg yolk and brush the tops of the cookies with the egg wash. Place the cookies 2 inches apart on ungreased cookie sheets. Sprinkle them generously with granulated sugar and bake for 5 to 7 minutes until they are light brown and a bit crispy. If they are not done, check at 1-minute intervals until they are.

Remove the cookies from the cookie sheets and allow them to cool. Dust with confectioners' sugar just before serving.

20 tablespoons (2½ sticks) butter
⅔ cup packed brown sugar
2 teaspoons finely grated lemon zest
1 teaspoon pure vanilla extract
6 egg yolks
2½ cups flour
1 teaspoon baking powder
½ teaspoon kosher salt
1 egg
¾ cup granulated sugar
Confectioners' sugar, for dusting

OLIVE OIL 101

or Fabio's All You Need to Know About Olive Oil

LET'S TALK ABOUT a primary staple in my cooking, olive oil. It's probably the item I reach for most in my pantry, and trust me I do use it—A LOT. When you find yourself in your favorite grocery store, staring at the endless shelves of olive oil, you may wonder how to choose the right one. If you're seeking simple, foolproof advice, here's mine. Bertolli® Olive Oil gives you several varietals for different uses, all at your fingertips.

OLIVE OIL IS KEY TO GREAT COOKING:

My food isn't complicated or pretentious, but it tastes fantastic because of time-tested, indispensible ingredients like Bertolli Olive Oil.

Did you know Bertolli has been making olive oil since 1865? Olive oil makes the best salad dressings and marinades. It's essential for caramelizing vegetables and sautéing almost everything. You need it to fry fish and chicken cutlets. It's "massaged" into chicken or beef (yes, I do massage my roasts with it) for roasting to seal in natural juices. Potatoes tossed with olive oil before roasting or baking come out crispier. Of course, you always add a little olive oil to pasta at serving time to prevent sticking and to provide better flavor. You can even use Bertolli Olive Oil in baking, as a replacement for butter at times, to provide moisture and consistent texture in breads, muffins, and cakes. I can't count the dishes that are not complete until you finish the dish with another hit of olive oil before serving.

ALWAYS CHOOSE A GOOD-QUALITY OLIVE OIL: Unlike wine, olive oil does not get better with time. Bertolli Olive Oil is known for its superior quality, as you'll find on its Extra Virgin Olive Oil label "first cold pressing" and on the back, its best if used by date. As soon as you get your olive oil home from the store, smell and taste it. You want a robust, almost grassy aroma, and a slightly spicy, peppery taste—that's Bertolli Extra Virgin Olive Oil. That said, you can save it for quite some time but olive oil needs to be kept in a dark place and away from heat. Be sure you protect this "juice of the gods" (yes, for me that's olive oil, not wine) from sunlight. If your new bottle of oil smells bad in any way, take it back to the store and ask for another.

HOW EXTRA VIRGIN OLIVE OIL IS MADE IS IMPORTANT: Cold pressing is the best process, meaning that the oil comes from pressing the olives instead of the cheaper way, which is extracting the oil by using heat or chemicals. The first press derives the purest flavor and preserves the health benefits.

DIFFERENT OLIVE OILS, DIFFERENT USES: Extra virgin olive oil is the highest grade for olive oil; because it's the one with the most noticeable peppery taste, this is what I use for drizzling, finishing, and making salad dressings and pasta sauces. My favorite among the Bertolli Olive Oil varietals is their selection of Extra Virgin Olive Oils, especially the Robusto, with a rich aroma and intense olive flavor that reminds me of the best oil I grew up with. When you're cooking something a long time, like a meat sauce, the one labeled "Classico Olive Oil" is versatile, with a medium taste great for sautéing and roasting. The "Extra Light Tasting" is great for high-heat cooking, such as frying and baking, because its mild flavor won't change with high heat.

YES, OLIVE OIL IS REALLY GOOD FOR YOU! First, it has more monounsaturated fat than other oils—that's the good fat, so it's powerful nutrition for your heart. Scientific research suggests that eating 2 tablespoons of olive oil may reduce the risk of coronary heart disease thanks to the MUFA (monounsaturated fatty acids) in olive oil, when it replaces a similar amount of saturated fat.

Second, unlike other edible oils such as seed oils, extra virgin olive oil is 100% natural, and contains polyphenols, strong natural antioxidants. Consumption of olive oil polyphenols helps protect blood lipids from oxidative damage which can cause cardiovascular diseases.

That's why people from my home are so healthy and live so long!

USE BERTOLLI OLIVE OIL INSTEAD OF BUTTER: Almost anytime your recipe calls for butter, try substituting olive oil.

- The rules of thumb are ¾ teaspoon olive oil in place of 1 teaspoon butter, which saves 1 fat gram and 10 calories;
- 3 tablespoons olive oil in place of ¼ cup butter, saving 12 fat grams and 110 calories; and
- ¾ cup olive oil in place of 1 cup butter, saving 48 fat grams and 430 calories.

NEW FROM BERTOLLI OLIVE OIL: You can find Bertolli Extra Virgin, Classico, and Extra Light Tasting also in sprays. You can also find my personal favorite oil, the Robusto, along with Fragrante and Gentile for cooks who want a more flavorful oil.

All information provided by Bertolli Olive Oil (a division of Deoleo, SA). All rights are reserved by Deoleo S.A. Author is a fee-based brand ambassador for Bertolli products.

MENUS FOR SPECIAL OCCASIONS

A Winter Holiday Meal

Rosemary and Pecorino Shortbread

Kale Salad with Mushrooms, Mozzarella, and Orange Segments

Roast Prime Rib of Beef with Best Little Yorkshire Puddings

Butternut Squash and Potato Salad from the Oven with Herb Dressing

Bean Casserole, Sun-dried Tomatoes and Parmesan Crust

Winter Squash Buns

Date and Lemon Ricotta Cake

A Sunday Family Supper

Ham-and-Cheese-Stuffed Pork Chops

Braised Collard Greens with Beans, Peperoncino, and Pancetta

Skillet Corn Bread

Pear-Hazelnut Tart

An Elegant Dinner Party

Grilled Asparagus with Burrata and Almond Salsa

Sautéed Sea Bass with Romesco Sauce

Whole Beef Tenderloin, Peppered and Grilled

Roasted Scalloped Potatoes with Creamy Sun-dried Tomato Pesto

Vanilla Fritters with Prosecco Cream

Brunch Menus

Open-Faced Zucchini Omelet

Parmesan Biscuits and Sausage Gravy

Fig, Strawberry, and Honey Butter

Poached Eggs with Espresso-Glazed Bacon

Squash Flapjacks with Basil Cream

Buttermilk and Black Pepper Biscuits

Chocolate Coffee Cake

A Simple Weeknight Dinner

Quick Chicken Parmigiana

Baby Potatoes Roasted in Parchment Paper

Italian Chocolate and Caramel Pudding

A Game Day Meal for the Guys

Italian Fried Missouri-Style Ravioli

Chunky Sausage and Clam Chowder

Philly Cheesesteak

Really Easy Mississippi Mud Pie

A Summer Picnic

Roasted Apricot Tapenade

Chilled Corn Soup with Parmesan-Basil
    Corn Salad

Fresh Tuna Salad Sandwiches

Grilled Green Tomatoes with Feta, Mint,
    and Basil

Grandma's Sugar Sprinkled Cookies

A Party Buffet

Fava Bean–Mint Hummus

Tomato Tart

Pork Roast Braised with Sweet Wine
    and Oranges

The Best Macaroni and Cheese with
    Parmesan Crumbs

Creamed Corn and Mozzarella

No-Knead Bread

Cheddar Cheese Apple Pie
    with a Hint of Parmesan

A Meal for Unexpected Guests

Parmesan or Pesto Crostini

Artichoke and Olive Spaghetti

or

Spaghetti with Quick Tuna Sauce

Chocolate Currant Cookies

ACKNOWLEDGMENTS

WHEN I FIRST MOVED TO AMERICA the last thing I would ever have believed is that one day, I'd become a *New York Times* best-selling author. Even less believable than that was that I would one day have the chance to publish a book about the food I love the most in this country. But here I am! God bless you all for all the support and love that you, the people of America, have shown me in so many ways. For all of it, let me say from the bottom of my little Italian heart: thank you.

Some people contributed even more to make it possible for me to publish a book like this. First and foremost Melanie Rehak, thank you, I'm not sure why you even want to work with me and keep translating my tortured English into something readable. I'll never understand, but all I can say is thank you. To my group at Hachette: Martha Levin, Sydny Miner, Shubhani Sarkar, and every single person on the team there who has worked so hard, I know how to cook and I know how to tell stories. I know nothing about editing or graphics so thank you, too, for all your amazing work. A special thanks to you, Martha, for trusting this crazy Italian guy in the publishing world.

John Paolone and Johnathan Lynch, thank you forever for helping with testing, tasting, and shopping with me for all the stuff for this book. We always have a blast together and you guys are a big part of the reason that everything I do is possible. A very warm thank you as well to my dear pastry chef Bambi Hosaka, for some help with something I'm not the best at, baking. I couldn't dream of a better team on my side.

Mike Langner, thank you for all your hard work in making sure that everything I do makes sense from a business standpoint and that we stay always ahead of the game. The reason I will never face prison due to some bad business decision is totally you.

Matt Armendariz: you, my man, are the reason why my food looks so good. Your photography and expertise in getting things done made this a flawless process and I just want to keep doing cookbooks so we can hang out together more often. You're nothing short of a miracle with a camera.

A big "Thank You" also to my team at Cafe Firenze for providing countless lunches and supplying all the tools to make the cooking part of creating this book a breeze, I love you guys.0

INDEX

"It's never about re-inventing the wheel—just making it spin faster and more deliciously than it did before."